THE MORAVIAN PRINCIPLE:

The Secret of Revival

THE MORAVIAN PRINCIPLE:

The Secret of Revival

DR. BRAD ALLEN

Printed in the United States of America

ISBN: 978-1-59571-993-5

Designed and published by:
Word Association Publishers
205 Fifth Avenue
Tarentum, Pennsylvania 15084
www.wordassociation.com
1.800.827.7903

PREFACE

When I began the research and study of the Moravians, I had no idea of the depth and length of their commitment to Jesus Christ. I was not fully aware of how they had marched across the world with the message of the gospel of Christ. When you sit back and think of the time in which they lived (1700s), it seems impossible that these people could go to some of the most forsaken places in the world to live. They went with no knowledge of the people, no training in the language of the people, no advance provision of what they would eat, where they would live, how they would operate. But, these men and women went with the firm determination that God had called them to this field, and He would take care of them.

In all that the Moravians did, you will find interwoven in their lives the secret to revival. The secret is the same that is revealed in the New Testament Church as those first disciples left the comfort of their home in Israel and went out across the then-known world to share the gospel of Christ.

During the writing of this book, there were periods in which I needed encouragement. In fact, I needed someone to goad me on to keep writing. I want to thank three people who reminded me of my responsibility of keeping on. I thank Greg Gordon of Canada, Richard Luke of Australia, and Gary Cannon of America for gently giving me encouragement as I wrestled with this study.

I also wish to give thanks to the Lord for placing this

study on my heart and keeping me on the right track as I studied about the wonderful Moravian people and their secret to revival.

FOREWORD

Brad Allen's challenging new work, "The Moravian Principle: The Secret to Revival", has as its title suggests two powerful themes. Firstly, a detailed study of the "principle" behind the Moravians' astounding revival beginning in 1727, And secondly, how this is the often concealed factor- the secret if you like- of God pouring out his Spirit in such a glorious and special way that not only is the church revived and transformed, but even an entire nation!

Brad brings to this work the same well-honed research and analytical skills that heralded his writings on the Hebrides Islands revival of 1949-53 as a new and exciting dimension in Christian revival literature.

But, because of the serious state of moral and spiritual unrest in the USA today, his latest magnum opus seems to carry even more weight as we address key question: Could another Moravian-style revival be the savior of America? Could the values and example of the Moravians who inspired such great moves of the Holy Spirit as the Wesleyan Revival under John Wesley not only transform society but shake the very foundations of western civilization? Could this be the prophesized revival before the return of the Lord Jesus Christ?

As Brad Allen observes America or any nation- as proven by the Moravians under the leadership of Count Zinzendorf- can become Kingdom movers and shakers by taking to heart in particular one all-powerful verse on the subject: "If My people, who are called by My name, shall humble themselves, and pray, and seek My face, and turn from their wicked ways; then will I hear from heaven, and will forgive their sin, and will heal their land." (II Chronicles 7:14)

Another vital aspect of Brad's new work is that not only can a Christian learn to be corporately part of a major revival- and this mainly through non-stop, persistent prayer- but he can privately draw closer to God the Father through Jesus by following the Moravians wonderful personal habits of prayer, study, meditation, fasting, confession and worship.

With this strong foundation of personal faith, the Moravians organized a twenty-four hour a day prayer chain in which at least two people were at prayer every hour of the day. This prayer meeting would last over 100 years and ultimately change the course of Christendom.

Will we witness again such sacrificial love and fervent prayer and seeking out of God's purposes?

Read Brad's inspired book to form your own answer.

Richard J. Luke
Founder/Editor
"Creative Words"
Editor
"Uniting Church: Powerful Moments"
Sydney, Australia

FOREWORD

Modern evangelical believers hardly know, sadly, of the Moravians. Very few church history books even mention them. Everyone is strangely quiet about what was one of the greatest apostolic expansions of the gospel- in purity and influence- since the Book of Acts. When asked to write the foreword to this volume, my heart leapt. After having read Moravian history for a few years, my heart burned afresh as I reviewed this volume that is clearly articulated and passionately proclaimed.

When one speaks of the Moravians and Count Zinzendorf, one must speak much of Jesus Christ and the wounds of the Lamb of God. Jesus Christ was the driving passion, heart and vision of the movement. Christ was the Leader, the King, and the Head of the Church. The Moravians even zealously had a special service to commemorate and proclaim Jesus Christ as Head of the growing Moravian Church. They traced the lineage of their movement back to the early Apostles through the old Bohemian Church. God was reviving the "hidden seed" of a succession of an apostolic order. There were no man-made agendas. Jesus Christ was the vision and all-consuming One.

If one were to go into a Moravian chapel, you could not escape see the Lamb of God in the window or centerpiece. They saw the Lord Jesus Christ as a bloodied conquering Lamb. What an ironic picture of the very Son of God who created the world reigning as a bloodied, wounded Lambkin. From the world's perspective, the Moravians were deluded, but that was their genius. They were caught up with the heavenly vision to preach the Good News of the Lamb to all who would hear. The great love of God was their message and His blood the answer. They believed in an all-sufficient Savior who satisfied God with His blood and was able to save the vilest to the Godhead.

For our modern minds, the thought of mediating on the blood and wounds of Christ seems even repulsive, yet to the Moravians it was joy and life. They basked in the wounded side of the Lamb and saw in Him their shelter. The way Moravian communities lived was radical in itself. They wore godly attire and separated much from the world's ways and fashions. They counted the cost to follow Christ and lived a life of denial of self.

The influence of the Moravians is un-told. They are chiefly God's secret movement. They were used of the Lord in-part for the conversions of George Whitfield, John Wesley, Charles Wesley and many other prominent preachers of that day. They provoked the English Christians to jealously which started what many call the modern missions movement with William Carey. But, what is un-told is that there were more Moravian missionaries active than all other sects of Christendom combined in their day. The Moravians did not confer with flesh and blood, but heard the voice of the Savior and left all to martyrs' deaths willingly in uttermost parts of the world. Even missions today are still catching up to some of the places the Moravians went and instilled the pure Gospel of the Son of God slain.

Sadly, the movement waned, but that took over 150 years for the embers to die out. The seed again is hidden in various sects and groupings of Christendom worldwide. Will God again revive that "hidden seed" and see a unified thrust of the body of Christ, His bride in the earth proclaiming the wounds of the Savior?

May God allow another great Unity of the Brethren to proclaim the riches of His great love. May the Lamb that was slain receive the reward of His sufferings.

Greg Gordon
Abbotsford, BC, Canada
Founder: www.sermonindex.net

CONTENTS

INTRODUCTION

Some ask the question, "What good does it do to delve into the past, looking at past revivals?" It does little good unless it creates within us a deep hunger and thirst that God might send gracious revival to us. In this book, you are going to be looking at the great revival, which happened among the Moravians. It is a startling, wonderful story of God coming down among a group of people.

On August 13, 1727 the Holy Spirit fell in mighty power on a little Moravian Church in Herrnhut, Germany. This one-day event, which came in such power, had a lasting effect of decades. In fact, that which God did on that day in Herrnhut is still producing results in our day.

To rightly understand this Moravian revival of 1727, we need to go back 300 years to find all the workings of God among these people.

The Moravian Church was founded over 500 years ago, and still remains a denomination today. The worldwide membership of the Moravians today is quite small. There is a Moravian settlement in Leeds, England; other Moravians are in a gathering in Tanzania in Africa. There are Moravian Churches in America. However, quite sadly, the Moravian Church today has slipped from its earlier hold on biblical truth. Today the Moravian Church has accepted many of the doctrines of modern thought and practice.

Perhaps, sometime or somewhere, you have come across the famous Moravian statement, which characterized their lives and their practices. That statement is, "In essentials, unity; in non-essentials, liberty; in all things, love."

There have been many wonderful tributes paid to the Moravians. G.A. Valerd, the historian said, "Moravians are the best Christians in the world." Oswald J. Smith said of Count Zinzendorf, the main organizer of the Moravians, "No man has been so mightily used of God since the days of the Apostle Paul." Ronald Knox, a Roman Catholic theologian, said, "The Moravians were the vital leaven of European Protestantism."

Will you join me as we go back 300 years before the Moravian Pentecost on August 13, 1727? This is necessary to fully understand all the things that God did in the lives of these dear people.

CHAPTER ONE

"THE TIMES OF JOHN HUSS"

The Moravians have been called by different names through the years. They were called the Church of the Brethren, the Bohemian Brethren, the Unitas Fratrum (Unity of the Brethren).

Bohemia has a vital, interesting history. In our modern geography, Bohemia is known as the Czech Republic. In the 14th century King Richard II of England married Princess Anne of Bohemia. Princess Anne brought a Bohemian Bible to England with her. A few years later, Bohemian scholars came to England to study at Oxford. They became acquainted with the writings of John Wycliffe. Wycliffe has been called, "The Morning Star of the Reformation." These scholars returned to Bohemia, taking the writings of Wycliffe with them, and his writings became a national sensation in the religious life of Bohemia. Wycliffe's writings became the foundation of the Bohemian Brethren.

Bohemia was the home of two populations; the native Czech and the intruding Germans. Bohemia was surrounded by Germany on three sides. On the northeast was Silesia, the northwest, Saxony, on the west Bavaria. On the southeast corner of Bohemia was the country of Moravia.

The early history of Bohemia contains a succession of bloody wars with Germany. The Germans settled in large numbers in the city of Prague. They brought in hundreds of

German clergymen, who preached in the German language. They introduced German laws into many of the towns. They made an attempt to make Germany the official language of Bohemia. They declared that the Bohemian language was only fit to be used by slaves. The Bohemian people hated the Germans with a passion. One said, "It is better for the land to be a desert than to be held by Germans; it is better to marry a Bohemian peasant girl than to marry a German queen." A Bohemian poet said that Judas Iscariot was probably a German.

This conflict between Bohemians and Germans also found its way into the religious life of Bohemia. Two preachers, Cyril and Methodius, had come from the Greek Church in Constantinople. They preached to the people in the Bohemian language. The German Archbishop of Salzburg brought in a number of German priests. The people loved the Greek preachers and hated the German priests. (1)

A number of preachers came to Bohemia in the 14th century, and had some effect on the people. Conrad of Waldhausen was in Bohemia from 1363-69. He denounced the sins of the clergy and the idle habits of the rich. He preached against the women of high society and told them to give up their fine dresses and jewels. He called well-known sinners to come and do penance in public.

Milic of Kremsin preached in Bohemia from 1363-74. He was a Bohemian and preached in the Bohemian language. He lived a life of self-sacrifice. He renounced his position as a Canon of the Church. He rescued thousands of fallen women, and built them homes. He was so disgusted with the conditions of the world that he was convinced the end of the world was coming soon. He preached in public that the Emperor, Charles IV, was the Anti-Christ, went to Rome and put a notice on the door of St. Peter's declaring the Anti-Christ had come. (2)

The next man who came along, and had an impact on the religious life of Bohemia was Thomas of Stitny (1370-1401) Thomas held up the Holy Bible as the standard of faith, wrote devotional books, and severely denounced the immorality of the monks. Thomas said, "The monks have fallen away from love. They have not the peace of God in their hearts; they quarrel, condemn and fight each other; they have forsaken God for money."

The three preachers I have mentioned were men of good character. They attacked the sins of the clergy and the luxury of the rich. They were all three loyal to the Roman Catholic Church.

But, then came Matthew of Janow (1381-93). For almost 40 years, from 1378-1414, there was a scandal that shocked the Roman Catholic Church. There occurred a division where there were two, and sometimes, three Popes. They spent these years fighting each other. There was Pope Urban VI, a thug, who had five of his enemies murdered. There was also Pope Clement VII, who was a scheming politician, and Pope John XXIII, who had a character not worth mentioning on the printed page.

The preacher, Matthew of Janow, was active in Bohemia during this time of schism. He lost confidence in the Catholic Church, and had a deep desire to return the church to the simple teachings of Christ and the Apostles. He wrote, "I consider it essential to root out all weakness, to restore the Word of God on earth, to bring back the Church of Christ to its original, healthy, condensed condition, and to keep only such regulations as date from the time of the Apostles. All the works of men, their ceremonies and traditions, shall soon be totally destroyed; the Lord Jesus shall alone be exalted, and His Word shall stand forever."

It was into this type of atmosphere that the writings of John Wycliffe came to Bohemia. Wycliffe had declared that the Pope was capable of committing a sin. He taught that the Pope was not to be obeyed unless his commands were in line with the teachings of the Bible. Wycliffe placed the authority of the Bible above the authority of the Pope. He denounced the whole sacrament system of the Catholic Church, and taught that man could come into contact with God without the aid of priests.

All that was needed in Bohemia was one man who would gather up all the dangling straws that were burning dimly in Bohemia, and bring them into one large bundle that would burn brightly for Jesus Christ in the land.

That one man was John Huss (Jan Hus). Huss was born in 1369 and died in 1415. He brought the reformation to Europe one hundred years before Martin Luther nailed his 95 theses to the church house door in Wittenberg. Huss was born in
Bohemia, which we call the Czech Republic today. He came from a poor family, but was able to get his education at Prague University. Huss studied the writings of John Wycliffe. He

found himself, more and more, preaching against the Roman Catholic Church of which he was a member.

For twelve years, John Huss was the boldest of all the reformers in Bohemia. He was a fine preacher, a very powerful writer, and became a popular hero to the people of Bohemia. Huss had entered the ministry, not because he wanted to do good, but in order to make a good living. He began as a very orthodox Catholic. He preached against the sins of all classes of people. A noble lady complained to the King. The King told the Archbishop of Prague to warn Huss to tone down his preaching. The Archbishop told the King, "No, Huss is bound by his ordination oath to speak the truth without respect of persons." (3)

Then, John Huss began to attack the sins of the clergy. Now the Archbishop complained to the King. The King told the Archbishop, "Nay, Hus is bound by his ordination oath to speak the truth without respect of persons."

The preaching of John Huss began to fan the desire of the people for reform, and also taught them to despise the clergy more than every.

Huss made a practice of preaching on the popular topics of the day, and the most popular topic was the power the Germans had in Bohemia. Huss said, "We Bohemians are more wretched than dogs or snakes. A dog defends the couch on which he lies. If another dog tries to drive him off, he fights him. A snake does the same. But us the Germans oppress. They seize the offices of state, and we are dumb. In France the French are foremost. In Germany the Germans are foremost. What use would a Bohemian bishop or priest, who did not know the German language, be in Germany? He would be as useful as a dumb dog, which cannot bark, to a flock of sheep. Of exactly the same use are German priests to us. It is against the law of God! I pronounce it illegal." (4)

King Wenceslaus declared that the Bohemians would be more fairly represented at Prague University. They now had three out of four votes. The people of Bohemia gave credit to John Huss for bringing about this change.

If Huss had stopped there, he would probably have gone to his death as one of the great men of the Roman Catholic Church, but he began to preach Wycliffe's doctrines in his sermons. The doctrines of Wycliffe had been condemned by the Roman Church and 200 of his books had been burned at Prague University. The Roman Church looked on Wycliffe as a heretic.

John Huss realized what his end would be. He knew if he kept preaching these doctrines, he would be burned at the stake. The Archbishop forbade him to preach in his pulpit at Bethlehem Chapel. Huss went on preaching. This was the time of the two rival Popes. The clergy was in a quandary; which Pope to recognize. John Huss would recognize neither. One of the Popes, John XXIII sent a group of priests to Prague to raise money so the Pope could raise an army to go to war with the King of Naples. The King of Naples supported the other Pope. The group of priests came to Prague to sell indulgences. They told the people if they would buy the indulgences, it would do two things; they would gain full forgiveness of their sins, and they would support the Pope in his campaign. John Huss was extremely angry. He did not believe in Pope John, nor did he believe in indulgences. Hus preached, "Let who will proclaim the contrary; let the Pope, or a Bishop, or a priest say, 'I forgive you your sins; I free you from the pains of hell.' It is all vain, and helps you nothing. God alone, I repeat, can forgive sins through Christ."

From this time forward, Huss became the leader of the national religious movement. During this time, three young men sang a song, "Priest, thou liest! The indulgences are a fraud." All three of the young men were beheaded on a street corner. Women dipped their handkerchiefs in their blood and one noble woman spread her fine linen over their bodies. Some of the students at Prague University picked up the bodies of the three young men and carried them to be buried in Bethlehem Chapel. At the head of this procession was John Huss. Hus conducted their funeral service. (5)

Now, the life of Huss was in danger. He left Prague, went to the castle of Kradonec in the country. He preached to huge crowds in the fields and wrote two books, which would bring him closer to the burning stake. His two books, "On Traffic in Holy Things", and "The Church", were critical of indulgences and the whole conception of the "Holy Catholic Church."

Sigismund, King of the Romans and of Hungary, asked Pope John XXIII to call a church council meeting at Constance. He invited John Huss to attend the council meeting to put forth his beliefs. Huss received from Sigismund a letter of "safe conduct." In the letter, he promised Huss three things; that he would come unharmed to the city, that he would have a free hearing, and that if he did not submit to the decision of the council he would be allowed to go home. Only the first of these promises was kept.

Huss was thrown into prison by the Pope, placed in a dungeon on an island in the Rhine River, and lay down next to a sewer. He stayed in this dungeon for three and one-half months, and then was moved to a castle on Lake Geneva. When he was finally called to appear before the Council, he found he had already been condemned as a heretic. The only change Huss had of living was to renounce the teachings of Wycliffe.

On the last day of his "trial", John Huss stood before the Council. It was a gruesome scene. For many weeks Huss had suffered. His face was pale, his cheeks were sunken, he was weak and trembling, but his voice rang clear and loud. Huss begged for a hearing, to be allowed to speak. The Council told him to be quiet. Huss was accused of teaching that he himself was the fourth person of the Godhead. Huss said, "Let that doctor be named who has given this evidence against me." The name of that accuser was never given. Now he was accused of a most dangerous error. He had appealed to God instead of appealing to the Church. Huss said, "O Lord God, this Council now condemns your action and law as an error! I affirm that there is no safer appeal than that to the Lord Jesus Christ."

When Huss said these words, he had signed his own death warrant. The Bishop of Concordia read out the articles of condemnation. The books of Huss were to be burned; his priestly office was to be taken from him, he was to be expelled from the Church, and handed over to the civil authorities.

As the sentence was read, Huss fell to his knees and began to pray, "Lord Jesus Christ, pardon all my enemies, I pray you, for the sake of Your great mercy! You know that they have falsely accused me. O, pardon them for Your infinite mercies' sake." (6)

The Church leaders who were present began to jeer at Huss. He was ordered to climb the scaffold, put on the priestly garments, and to recant his beliefs. He did mount the scaffold, he did put on his priestly garments, but he refused to recant any of his beliefs.

Huss stood on the scaffold in his long white robe and cried out, "Behold, these Bishops demand that I recant and abjure. I dare not do it. If I did, I would be false to God, and sin against my conscience and Divine truth." (7)

The Bishops snatched the Communion Cup from his hand and cried, "Thou cursed Judas! You have forsaken the council of peace. You have become one of the Jews. We take from you this Cup of Salvation." Hus replied, "But I trust in God Almighty, and shall drink this Cup this day in His Kingdom."

The Bishops then took his robe from him. They took scissors and cut his hair, and place a fool's cap on his head. They began to march Huss down the street to his place of execution. One thousand soldiers marched along, with a huge crowd of supporters lining the streets. They came to the place, a meadow outside the city gates. At the stake, Huss knelt once more in prayer; the fool's cap fell from his head. He was bound to the stake with seven moist ropes and a rusty chain. Wood and straw were piled around him from his feet to his chin. Once again he was approached and given one last chance to recant.

Huss shouted out, "What errors shall I renounce? I know myself guilty of none. I call God to witness that all that I have written and preached has been with the view of rescuing souls from sin and perdition, and therefore most joyfully will I confirm with my blood the truth I have written and preached."

The flame was lit, the wood began to crackle. His lips moved in silent prayer, and in a few minutes he breathed no more. When the fire died down, the soldiers took his remains from the stake, hacked his skull in pieces, and ground his bones into powder. As they poked around in the fire, they found that his heart was still unburned. One put his heart on the point of a spear, jabbed it back into the fire and watched it burn away. They gathered up all the ashes, and threw everything in the Rhine River.

John Huss died that day, but his cause was just beginning to live.

CHAPTER TWO

"AFTER JOHN HUSS"

When the ashes of John Huss sank beneath the waters of the Rhine River, the news of his murder spread across Bohemia like wildfire. Huss had been the national hero of the people. He was looked upon as a saint by the common people. A Hussite League was formed by his friends and a Catholic League was formed by his enemies. Then the Hussite Wars started.

When a movement is started, it can grow and expend if it has its leader. Without John Huss, his followers soon began to form splinter groups; some believed one thing, some believed another.

One of the groups of the followers of Huss was the Utraquists or sometimes called the Calixtines. They emphasized one of the doctrines that John Huss had taught, that laymen should be permitted to take the wine at the Communion. They became very bitter in fighting for this doctrine.

Another group was the Taborites. They very extremely radical, and had ideas of Socialism with regard to property and were very loose in their morals. They rejected the Catholic teachings of purgatory, masses, the worship of saints, condemned images, relics and fasting. They believed priests were a nuisance and they baptized their babies in ponds. They felt that every person had a right to his own belief about the Bible, and they practiced tearing down churches and burning monks to death.

The Chiliasts was another group that came from the ministry of John Huss. They believed that the end of the world was at hand, and the millennial reign of Christ would begin very soon. They were waiting for a signal from heaven to start a massacre of their fellow men. But, that signal never came to them.

Another small group was the Adamites. They were called this because they went about naked as Adam and Eve did before their fall into sin.

Another group was the Waldenses. They were an old group, having come from Italy about sixty years before. They held that prayer should not be addressed to the Virgin Mary, but to God alone. They did attend the public worship services of the Roman Catholic Church, but they did not believe in those services. They did not build churches, but felt that a person could worship God in the field or meadow as well as in a building. They totally rejected purgatory, and believed a person would go to either heaven or hell. The Waldenses believed that the Roman had become totally corrupt. It may well be that in the teachings of the Waldenses; we might see the one great principle that laid the foundation for the Moravian Church. The Waldenses believed they must return to the simple teachings of Jesus Christ and His Apostles. The Waldenses laid strong emphasis on the Sermon on the Mount. They believed war was murder, that the law of Christ was supreme. They called each other brother and sister.

Pope Martin V announced a crusade war against the people of Bohemia. For the next twenty years the land was a boiling mass of slaughter Out of this mass of smoking runs, the Moravian Church had its beginning. One of the groups that had been followers of John Huss saw that radical reform in the Roman Catholic Church was not going to happen. They decided to set up their own worshipping community. They moved to another part of Bohemia in 1457 and set up this little community that believed in Christ, worshipped Him in simplicity and practiced the celebration of the Lord's Supper by giving both bread and wine to Christians who came to the Lord's Table.

Within three years this little group had grown to such numbers that they needed three bishops to look after them. Before that century was over, there were 200,000 of these simple Christians in Bohemia. At that time they took the name, Unitas Fratrum (Unity of the Brethren). They became known as the Bohemian Brethren or the Church of the Brethren. (1)

CHAPTER THREE

"THE APOSTLE PETER OF THE 15TH CENTURY"

During the 15th century, a prophet of God arose with a wonderful, challenging message. His name was Peter, and he lived in the small village of Chelcic. Very little is known about his life. What we know of Peter of Chelcic, we know from his writings. We do know that he studied the works of John Wycliffe and John Huss. He also knew the teachings of Jesus Christ in a most vivid way. He wrote in the Bohemian language. Peter of Chelcic appealed to the common people of Bohemia. The more he studied and observed the culture of his country, the more he came to the conclusion that the whole system of religion and politics in Bohemia were rotten to the core. He looked at the all the sects that had risen after the death of John Huss, and he saw in each one the bloody stain of murder. He could not find one of them that were true to the teachings of Jesus Christ

Peter's most famous writing was, "Net of Faith." In this work he said, "Through his disciples Christ caught the world in the net of His faith, but the bigger fishes, breaking the net, escaped. Then others followed through these same holes made by the big fishes, and the net was left almost empty." The people understood his meaning. The net was the true Church of Jesus Christ; the two big fish who broke it were the Roman Emperor and the Pope. The big fish were the mighty, learned people, and the little fish were the true followers of Christ. (1)

Peter of Chelcic laid out his teachings in a very clear manner.

The teaching of Jesus Christ and the Apostles was enough. This teaching was final, perfect and supreme.

If a king, or a Pope, or Council of Bishops made a new law, they were spoiling the teachings of Jesus Christ.

As Christ submitted to Pilate, so Christians must submit to government, but the less Christians had to do with government, the better.

Christians must never take each other to court.

Christians must never live in a town. He looked upon towns as abodes of evil

Peter strongly objected to the union of church and state. Peter said, "For three hundred years the Church of Christ had remained true to her Master, and then this disgusting heathen Emperor, Constantine, who had not repented of a single sin poisoned all the springs of the church's life. He was a ravenous beast; he was a wolf in the fold; he was a lion squatting at the table. In that fatal moment when he gave his "donation" to the Pope, an angel in heaven spoke the words, 'this day has poison entered the blood of the Church." (2)

Peter of Chelcic wrote and spoke viciously of the priests. He said they were immoral, superstitious, ignorant, empty-headed, instead of feeding the Church of God, they were starving the church to death. He accused the priests of loose teaching and shameless winking at sin. . Peter said, "I do not know of a single person whom they have helped with their learning."

Peter always mentioned the Waldenses with respect.

They are some who believe that he was a member of the Waldenses himself.

What did Peter of Chelcic believe? He believed in the redemptive value of the death of Christ on the cross. He believed that man must build all his hope, not on his own good works, but totally on the grace of God. He believed that good works were necessary and would receive their reward.

As the years passed, people in several of the towns of Bohemia began to accept Peter of Chelcic as their spiritual teacher. They read his writings. They became known as the, "Brethren of Chelcic." These began to dress alike with a grey cloak with a cord tied around the waist. This movement began to grow and grow. We do not know when Peter was born, nor do we know when he died. He came on the scene, delivered his message, showed the way. He began to shine a light in all the dark places of Bohemia. Whether Peter knew it or not, he laid the foundation for the Brethren Church. Peter of Chelcic had placed the dynamite of the gospel of Jesus Christ in Bohemia, now it needed someone to detonate the charge. That man is coming on the scene.

CHAPTER FOUR

"THE BEGINNING OF THE CHURCH OF THE BRETHREN"

The time period is 1457-1473. John Rockycana, the Archbishop of Prague, was creating quite a scene in that city. He was preaching, with unusual force, the teachings of Peter of Chelcic. He said that the Church of Rome was like a burned, ruined city. At one point, he said, from the pulpit, "It is better to tie a dog to a pulpit than allow a priest to defile it. It is better for your sons to be hangmen than to be priests; for the hangman only kills the body, while the priest kills the soul." One Sunday, while preaching, he suddenly looked at a picture of St. Peter on the wall, pointed to it, and said, "There is as much difference between the priests of today and the twelve apostles as there is between the old painting and the living St. Peter in heaven, for the priests have put the devil into the sacraments themselves, and are leading you straight to the fires of hell."

However, there was one thing wrong with John Rockycana. What he was preaching from the pulpit, he was unwilling to carry out in real life. The preaching of Peter of Chelcic had convinced many people of Bohemia that the only natural course to their new beliefs was to leave the Roman Church, never to return to it again. These people pled with John Rockycana to lead them out of the Roman Church, but he refused. He told the people, "I know you are right, but if I joined your ranks I would be reviled on every hand."

The people turned their back on John Rockycana and a large number of them left the Roman Church. In their group, they found another leader, whose name was Gregory. He became known as Gregory the Patriarch. He became the literally founder of the Church of the Brethren.

Gregory was already middle-aged. He was the son of a Bohemian knight. He had spent his youth as a Catholic monk, and had found the group of monks an immoral group. He left in disgust. He became known in Bohemia as a man of wonderful character, holy and sensible, a good writer and a sterling speaker. He had been a personal friend of Peter of Chelcic, and had studied his writings extensively.

Gregory finally lost patience with John Rockycana, left the church where John was preaching, and got in touch with little groups of believers in the towns of Wilenow and Divischau. He slowly began to form in his own mind the idea of forming an independent group of believers. The numbers of people around Gregory began to grow, and finally they were confronted with the question; where are we going to live. The answer they gave to that question would mean whether they lived or died.

In 1457, Uladislaus Postumus, King of Bohemia, died and George Podiebrad became King. At this time Gregory the Patriarch became aware of a little village in the northeast corner of Bohemia named Kunwald. This village was almost deserted. A few people of like belief of Gregory lived there. John Rockycana went to King George with the request that this group be permitted to move to Kunwald and it was granted. Gregory and his faithful people made their way to

Kunwald and there began to establish the first settlement of the Church of the Brethren.

Life was simple in the Valley of Kunwald for this group of believers. Their devotion was to Jesus Christ as King and to the Bible. They wrote a note back to John Rockycana, "As we knew not where to turn, we turned in prayer to God Himself, and besought Him to reveal to us His gracious will in all things. We wanted to walk in His ways; we wanted instruction in His wisdom; and in His mercy. He answered our prayers."

They chose Michael Bradacius as their Pastor. He had formerly been an Utraquist priest. They appointed twenty-eight elders. They divided themselves into three classes, the Beginners, the Learners and the Perfect. They settled town in Kunwald to live quiet, peaceable lives. Their only purpose was to live by their individual trades, study the Bible and live unblemished lives in the sight of God. (1)

A story reached the ears of King George that this small group in Kunwald was dangerous, and holding secret meetings. About the same time, Gregory the Patriarch came to Prague to talk to the University students. King George gave orders that all were to be arrested. The students avowed that would stand firm in the face of this persecution. That night the law enforcement officers descended on the meeting and arrested all of them. The students and Gregory were stretched on the rack. Most of the students lost their devotion, marched to the Thein Church, mounted the pulpit, one at a time, pled guilty to the charges that had been brought against them, and pledged their full belief in the teachings of the Holy Church of Rome. Gregory was now quite old. His wrists had broken on the rack, and he fainted. They thought he was dead. In his unconscious state, Gregory had a dream. He was in a meadow. There was a tree with much fruit. The fruit was being eaten by birds. These birds were being guided by a young person of heavenly beauty, and the tree was guarded by three men. Later the Church of the Brethren interpreted this dream in this way: the tree was the Church of the Brethren, the fruit was her Bible teaching, the birds were her ministers, the youth of great beauty was Jesus Himself, and the three men who stood guard were those three who were later selected as the first three Elders of the Brethren Church.

While Gregory was suffering so badly from this experience, John Rockycana, hearing that he was dying, came to visit with him. He told Gregory, "Oh, my Gregory, would I were where you are." When Gregory recovered, Rockycana made supplication to the King in his behalf, and King George allowed Gregory to return to the valley of Kunwald.

Then, serious persecution began for the Brethren. King George declared that he would only recognize the Roman Church and the Utraquist Church. Any who worshipped otherwise would be put to death. For two long years the Brethren lived their lives in the forests, living like wild animals as they were hunted by the authorities. They only dared cook their meals at night. When food ran low, they would march in single file to a village, dragging a branch in the snow behind them to hide their footprints. They read their Bibles in the forests, moved almost daily, but leaned heavily on the promise that where two or three were gathered together in His name, He was there in their midst. They made an appeal to John Rockycana, but he had gone over to the other side and would not help them in any way. The people of that area began to call them, "Pitmen", because they lived in caves and pits.

Now the time had come! A deep, excruciating decision had to be made. The Brethren had left the Roman Church, but they had settled on an estate owned by the Utraquists, they were living under the protection of a Utraquist King, they were attending church services conducted by a Utraquist priest. They began to ask themselves questions. Why should they listen to sermons preached by men in league with the state? Why should they take Bread and Wine from the hands of Utraquist priests? Why should they confess their sins to priests who had the shadow of Rome over their heads?

The Brethren began to form in their own hearts and minds their thoughts of what they wanted to do, and what would be the will of God for their lives. They wanted priests who were pastors, who would feed the people with spiritual knowledge and understanding. They wanted a church that had descended from the twelve Apostles. They wanted priests who would work with their hands for a living. Where could they find such men? For a time they were of the mind to just do without priests. They began to inquire in other countries concerning priests. They inquired about the Nestorian Church in India, but found that church was as bad as the church in Rome. They inquired about the Russian Orthodox Church, but found they were willing to consecrate any priest as long as he would pay the fees.

Martin Lupac, an Utraquist priest told the Brethren, "You must establish a proper order of priests from among yourselves. If you don't, the whole cause will be ruined. To do without priests is no sin against God; but it is a sin against your fellow men." (2)

This statement seemed to light a fire in the midst of the Brethren. They suddenly realized that they were growing all over Bohemia. They had the truth of Jesus Christ in their midst. They realized that if they were to continue, they must forever cut any ties to Rome and launch out on their own.

In 1467, ten years after the founding of their little group in Kunwald, the Brethren met in a Synod of the Brethren at Lhota. One question was paramount at this meeting, "Is it God's will that we separate entirely from the power of the Papacy, and hence from its priesthood? Is it God's will that we institute, according to the model of the Primitive Church, a ministerial order of our own?" (3)

They met in a tanner's cottage and prayed and fasted for several days. The day of decision came. Sixty men were on their knees in prayer. This group of men nominated by ballot nine men of blameless life, from whom would be chosen the first Pastors of the new church. Next twelve slips of paper were folded and put into a vase. Of these slips nine were blank, and three were marked "Jest" which is the Bohemian word for, "is." Then a boy named Procop entered the room, drew out nine slips and handed them to the nine nominated Brethren.

A great silence fell over the room. There were three

slips of paper left in the vase. It was agreed that the names on the remaining three slips of paper would be ordained to the gospel ministry. Matthias of Kunwald, Thomas of Prelouic, and Elias of Chrenouic have come down in history as the first three ministers of the Brethren Church. Gregory the Patriarch stepped forward and said these three men were the very ones he had seen in his dream when he was in the torture chamber in Prague.

Everyone at the meeting accepted, wholeheartedly, the three men. The next day they all sang a hymn, which had been written for the occasion.

> We needed faithful men, and He
> Granted us such, most earnestly,
> We pray, Lord, let Thy gifts descend,
> That blessing may Thy work attend.

For these three Pastors to be recognized, the Brethren felt they had to be ordained by a Bishop of pure descent from the Apostle. For this task, they chose Stephen, a Bishop of the Waldenses. In the past, Stephen had told the Brethren of the line of Bishops or Pastors who ran all the way back to the early church. He had told them that the Waldenses had never broken the teachings of Christ by uniting with the Roman Church. The Brethren sent Michael Bradacius to see Stephen in Southern Moravia. The old Bishop, Stephen, broke out in tears, laid his hand on Michael's head, and consecrated him as a Bishop. Michael returned and ordained the chosen three as Priests.

Gregory the Patriarch wrote a letter to King George

and told him that they were finished with the Church of Rome. Gregory, now in his old age, urged the Brethren to regulate their lives by the Sermon on the Mount. The Church of the Brethren saw in the Sermon on the Mount six commandments they had to follow:

No Brother could serve as a judge or magistrate.

No Brother could take an oath or keep an inn, or trade beyond the barest needs of life.

No nobleman, unless he relinquished his rank, could become a member of the Brethren Church.

No peasant could serve in the military or act as a bailiff on a farm.

No Brother could ever divorce his wife.

No Brother could every take any kind of action in a court of law. (4)

Gregory never became a Bishop. He remained a layman until his death in 1473. He is buried at Brandeis-on-the-Adler on the Moravian border

CHAPTER FIVE

"LUKE OF PRAGUE"

Before Gregory the Patriarch died in 1473, he said to one of the three Pastors chosen to lead the Brethren Church, "Ah, Matthias, beware of the educated Brethren!" Those words of warning proved to be true for the church.

When the Brethren Church was first forming in the Kunwald Valley, the larger number of its adherents were peasants and tradesmen of the poorer classes. As the years began to pass, numbers of rich and influential people began to come into the church. A large colony of Waldenses immigrated from Brandenburg in 1480 and joined the Brethren Church. University professors came into the church.

For many years the Brethren had followed strictly the teachings of Peter of Chelcic. For years one of the rules that had been followed was the one that said if a nobleman joined the Brethren Church, he must first lay down his rank. Now that rule was beginning to cause a problem. Men who were in positions of great trust in the government, men who were judges and held state offices were coming into the church. The Church felt forced to relinquish this rule, which they began to consider as a very narrow idea of Peter of Chelcic.

About this time there entered the Church a young man named, Luke of Prague. Luke was born in 1460. He was a well-read theological scholar, and for the next fifty years he was a respected and trusted leader of the Brethren Church.

Luke of Prague, along with a friend of his, Procop

of Neuhaus, became the leaders of a new movement in the Brethren Church.

Luke was the leader of this new movement, but on the other side was the "little party" which was made up of the old-fashioned, rigid people led by two farmers, Amos and Jacob. The "little party" wanted the Church to stay true to the teachings of Peter of Chelcic. The larger part of the Church, led by Luke of Prague, resolved that the teachings of Peter and Gregory would no longer be considered as binding on the Church. In 1494, a Synod was held at Reichenau at which they rejected the authority of Peter of Chelcic entirely. At this Synod they agreed that noblemen would join the church, that if a man's business was honest he could make a profit, that Brethren could enter a job in service to the state, and that oaths could be taken in certain circumstances. The following year, 1495, the Brethren Church came out with a very clear teaching. They now said that instead of taking Peter of Chelcic as their guide, they now took as their guide, the Bible, and the Bible alone.

So, now we can see quite clearly that forty years before John Calvin, and eighty years before Martin Luther, the Brethren Church declared that the words of Holy Scripture would be their only standard of faith and practice. From this time forward, the followers of Peter of Chelcic were not the Brethren, but the "little party" led by Amos and Jacob.

This new movement went further still. Peter of Chelcic had leaned more heavily on good works than on the doctrine of grace. At a meeting of the Council of Elders of the Brethren Church, Procop of Neuhaus raised a question,

"By what is a man justified?" Out of this meeting, the great doctrine of justification by grace was formed. Many believe that because of this high teaching that salvation is totally by the grace of God that the Brethren Church became the first organized Evangelical Church in Europe.

Luke of Prague began to change many things. He enlarged the number of Bishops and became a Bishop himself. He introduced golden communion cups and embroidered cloths into the Lord's Supper. Some thought he was leading them back to the Roman Church. Of the five printing presses in Bohemia, three belonged to the Brethren. Between 1500 and 1510 sixty printed works appeared and the Brethren wrote fifty of these. Luke edited the first Brethren's hymnbook in 1501. He wrote a commentary on Psalms, the Gospel of John, I Corinthians, chapter 11, and drew up the Confessions of Faith for the Church.

Luke and some others had a deep desire to have fellowship with others who believed as they did. Several of them set off to search for Brethren in other lands. One of the men went to find the pure Nestorian Church that was supposed to exist in India. He got as far as Antioch, Jerusalem and Egypt. He returned home with the notion that the River Nile flowed from the Garden of Eden, but he returned with no knowledge of the Church in India. Another of the Brethren went to South Russia. Another went seeking Christians in Turkey. Luke went to the monasteries of Greece and on to Rome. Luke wandered the streets of Rome, shocked at the sights he saw. He saw the streets littered with the dead bodies of men who had been murdered by Caesar Borgia. He saw

Savonarola put to death in Florence. Luke returned home absolutely disgusted, and was convinced that there was not a true Christian Church on the face of the earth except the Brethren.

It was good that Luke of Prague decided to return home, for there was trouble on the horizon for the Brethren Church. The town of Jungbunzlau was the headquarters of the Brethren Church. In this town lived a young man named, John Lezek. He became a member of the Brethren Church, and then decided if he could just invent some stories about the Brethren he could become very popular. He went to the Roman Catholic Priest of the parish and confessed to him a large number of things to him about the Brethren Church. He told the priest that he had robbed his own father with the consent of the Church, that the Brethren took the Communion Bread home with them and chopped it to pieces, that he had robbed many houses for them, and that they murdered men and kidnapped their wives. He told the priest that they had tried to kill John Rockycana with gunpowder, that they climbed up poles naked like Adam and Eve, that they were skilled in witchcraft, that they worshipped Beelzebub, and said the way to hell was paved with the baldheads of priests.

The Roman priest wrote all of this down, had witnesses sign it, copied it and began to scatter these tales across the nation. Soon John Lezek confessed before a judge that this entire story was false, but the stories kept on spreading.

At this time the Roman Pope was Alexander VI. One said of this Pope that he was the most successful image of the devil. He was greedy, immoral, and fond of pleasure. It was a known fact that he would poison people who got in his way. If a popular person in Rome died suddenly, the people took it for granted that Pope Alexander poisoned him. Pope Alexander set out strict measures against the Church of the Brethren. He was told that the number of Brethren was now over 100,00 members. He issued a Papal Bull in 1500, resolving to crush them to powder.

The Pope sent Dr. Henry Institoris to Moravia to carry out his threats. When he arrived in Moravia he was horrified to learn that most of the Brethren could read. He sent word to the Pope that they had learned this art from the devil. Dr. Ausustin Kasebrot sent word to King Uladislaus, "They are not even good enough to be burned at the stake. They ought to have their bodies torn by wild beasts and their blood licked up by dogs."

King Uladislaus issued an order, the Edict of St. James in 1508. In this edict, all meetings of the Brethren, both public and private, were forbidden. All books of the Brethren were to be burned. Anyone who lived in Bohemia who did not worship and join the Utraquist or Roman Catholic Churches would be driven from the country, and all priests and teachers of the Brethren would be thrown into prison.

Severe persecution began! One episode of one man has come down to us through history. His name was Andrew Poliwka, one of the Brethren who lived in the town of Kuttenburg. He attended the Roman Church to please his wife. When the sermon had closed and the priest lifted the bread and wine, Andrew could keep quiet no longer. He stood and shouted out, "Silence, Parson Jacob, you have babbled

enough! My hour is come; I will speak. Dear friends, what
are you doing? What are you adoring? An idol made of
bread! Oh! Adore the living God in heaven! He is blessed for
evermore." The priest ordered him to be quiet. He shouted
louder. He was caught, his head dashed against a pillar, and
he was dragged off to prison, bleeding badly. The next day
he was hauled into court and asked to explain himself. He
answered the court, "Who caused Abraham to forsake his
idolatry and adore the living God? Who induced Daniel to
flee from idols?" He was placed on the rack, burned at the
stake. As the flames began to gather around him, Andrew
cried out, "Jesus, Thou Son of the living God, have mercy
upon me, miserable sinner." (1)

For six years the persecution was extremely intense
for the Brethren. The churches were empty, the Pastors of
those churches were homeless, the people were scattered.
The Pastors had to hold services in the forests, hiding in can-
yons and valleys.

During this time of persecution, Luke of Prague was
the Bishop of these people. He remained faithful to the cause
of Christ in every respect. One day Luke of Prague was traveling to make a pastoral visit when he was captured by Peter
von Suda. He was bound with chains, thrown into a dungeon. The cause of the Brethren had sunk to its lowest ebb.
Some of the Brethren began to complain that there was no
hope. At their lowest point, suddenly several of the enemies
of the Brethren died. Dr. Augustin, a fierce foe, fell dead from
his chair at dinner. Baron Colditz fell ill of a carbuncle in his
foot, and died. Baron Henry von Neuhaus, who had boasted

to the King how many Brethren he had starved to death, was out driving his sleigh. The sleigh turned over and the Baron's hunting knife went through him and killed him. Baron Puta von Swihow was found dead in his cellar

Word began to spread that anyone who was tired of life should persecute the Brethren, then they would not live another year. The King of Bohemia, Uladislaus II, died on March 13, 1516. Luke of Prague was set free from the dungeon, and was selected as the Chief Elder of the Brethren. Fast on the heels of all of this, the whole country of Bohemia was in disorder. The Catholic Church and Utraquist Church were fighting with each other. The barons and knights began to fight with one another. Surprisingly, in the midst of all this turmoil, the Brethren were able to live in peace.

The year was 1517. Like a lightning bolt from heaven, word came to the Brethren that they were not alone. In this year Martin Luther nailed his 95 theses to the church house door at Wittenberg, Germany. For a period of time it seemed as if Martin Luther would have as much influence in Bohemia as

he did in Germany. Luther wrote a letter to the Bohemian Diet and urged the leaders in Prague to break all ties with the Roman Church.

The Brethren Church of Bohemia sent two German Brethren to see Luther. Their names were John Horn and Michael Weiss. They gave to Luther a copy of the Brethren Confession and Catechism. The Church of the Brethren was very anxious to converse with Luther and to build a bridge of understanding with him.

Luke of Prague died on December 11, 1528. Luke of Prague could never rest easy with the teachings of Martin Luther. Luke believed in the seven sacraments, the Brethren's system of moral discipline, and the celibacy of the clergy. Luke wrote, "This eating, this drinking, this self-indulgence, this marrying, this living to the world, what a poor preparation it is for men who are leaving Babylon. If a man does this he is yoking himself with strangers. Marriage never made anyone holy yet. It is a hindrance to the higher life, and causes endless trouble." Luke also was deeply troubled by the teaching of Martin Luther on the doctrine of justification by faith.

On one occasion, Luke wrote a letter to Luther on this doctrine of justification by faith, "Never, never can you ascribe a man's salvation to faith alone. The Scriptures are against you. You think that in this you are doing a good work, but you are really fighting against Christ Himself and clinging to an error." (2)

CHAPTER SIX

"A BEND IN THE ROAD"

If you are reading this book right now, you may be asking yourself the question, "When is the Moravian Pentecost coming?" Let me assure you that it is coming. I just believe it is necessary that we go back 300 years so we can build the correct foundation on that which the Moravians accomplished. We started with John Huss, looked at the teachings of Peter of Chelcic, took a glimpse at the life of Gregory the Patriarch, and learned of the life and teachings of Luke of Prague.

Now, the Church of the Brethren has come to a bend in the road. Their direction is taking a turn toward Germany. In 1517 Martin Luther nailed his 95 theses to the door of the church in Wittenberg, Germany, and Europe is about to undergo a radical change.

The Brethren in Bohemia called themselves, "Jednota Bratrska", the Church of the Brethren. They held a Synod in 1464, at which meeting they issued the following statement, "Above all things we are one in this purpose. We hold fast the faith of the Lord Christ. We will abide in the righteousness and love of God. We will trust in the living God. We will do good works. We will serve each other in the spirit of love. We will lead a virtuous, humble, gentle, sober, patient and pure life; and thereby shall we know that we hold the faith in truth, and that a home is prepared for us in heaven. We will show obedience to one another, as the Holy Scriptures command.

We will take from each other instruction, reproof and punishment, and thus shall we keep the covenant established by God through the Lord Jesus."

Probably because of what the Brethren had seen through the years in the lives of the Roman priests and monks, the Brethren were very careful in choosing whom they would ordain. Their chief requirement in ministers was not theological learning, but personal character. As long as a man lived a holy life and could preach to the people the simple truths of the Bible, the Brethren Church felt nothing else was required. They did not expect their ministers to know Greek and Hebrew. On one occasion, Martin Luther wrote a letter to the Brethren, urging them to take more interest in learning and knowledge. They wrote back to Luther these words, "We have no need of teachers who understand other tongues, such as Greek and Hebrew. It is not our custom to appoint ministers who have been trained at advanced schools in languages and fine arts. We prefer Bohemians and Germans who have come to a knowledge of the truth through personal experience and practical service, and who are therefore qualified to impart to others the piety they have first acquired themselves. And here we are true to the law of God and the practice of the early Church." (1)

The Brethren also had a rigid rule that all ministers would earn their living by manual labor. For his work as a Pastor, he never received a dime. A minister also could not marry without the consent of the Elders. They looked on a minister who did marry with disfavor. They felt he was guilty of the weakness of the flesh

The minister of a church was not looked upon as a ruler, but as a servant. He was not allowed to select his own topics for sermons, but had to preach on the Scripture appointed for that particular day. He had no home of his own, but lived in the Brethren's House with other ministers in training. If a boy desired to become a minister, he would move into the Brethren's House , taught a trade, and learn from other ministers. The Bohemian Brethren have never had any theological colleges.

In the Brethren's House were the Priest himself, the Deacons and the Acolytes.

The Deacons would preach in outlying areas, assisted at Holy Communion, took care of the distribution of alms, and did manual labor.

The Acolytes were young men or boys who were preparing to be Deacons. They rang the bells and lighted the candles in the Church, and took turns conducting household worship.

No one could leave the house without permission from the Pastor, and the Pastor could not leave without permission from the Bishop.

One of the things that set the Brethren apart from other members of the Bohemian society was their ability to read. Among the common people of Bohemia, very few could read, while, among the Brethren, there were very few who could not read.

The people of Bohemia began to hear tales and believe that the devil himself was teaching the Brethren to read. Baron Rosenberg said, "Is it really true that the devil teaches all who become Picards to read, and that if a peasant leaves the Brethren he is no longer able to read?" (2)

Instead of laying the blame of the ability to read on the devil, it would be more correct to place the ability to read on Luke of Prague. Luke had written,
"The Catechism for Children." Among the Brethren, this writing was commonly called, "The Children's Questions." Every father in every Brethren family used this book to teach his children. As children grew up in the Brethren Church, they learned to read, at church and in their own home. Fathers were to teach their children to read, to pray and to be righteous in their character. The father was to see that brothers and sisters were not to sleep in the same room. The father was not to strike his children with a stick or his fists. He was to teach his children the Catechism written by Luke of Prague.

The rules of conduct in the Brethren Church were very strict. The Brethren were noted as people who were very kind and extremely tenderhearted. Their homes were places of happiness and peace. They had offerings a few times each year for the poor. If a member of the church transgressed any of the rules, there were three steps involved in recovery of that person. For the first offense, the person was admonished in private. For the second offense, the person was rebuked in front of the Elders and excluded from Communion until repentance came. For the third offense, the person was denounced in front of the Church, then, when the whole congregation shouted, "Amen", that signaled the person's banishment from the Brethren Church.

The Brethren Church differed radically from the Roman Church and also the teaching of Martin Luther concerning the doctrine of the Lord's Supper. They totally denied the teaching of Transubstantiation, which the Catholic Church espoused, that the bread was turned into the actual body of Christ, and the wine was turned into the actual blood of Christ. They also rejected the teaching of Martin Luther, which was the doctrine of Consubstantiation. The Brethren came to much the same position as John Wycliffe had in England two hundred years before. The Brethren believed that Christ was present bodily at the right hand of God; that He was present spiritually in the heart of every believer; and that He was present sacramentally, but not personally, in the bread and wine.

The Brethren also differed from Martin Luther in the doctrine of Infant Baptism. The Brethren believed that no child could be a believer until he had been taught the faith . They did not believe in baptismal regeneration.

During this time, under the leadership of Luke of Prague, the Church of the Brethren indeed had reached a bend in the road. During this time they underwent a time of severe persecution, they hammered out many of their own beliefs and doctrines, they settled many of their thoughts about church leadership, and came to rest on the sanctity of the home. They were probably not aware of it at the time, but their faces were beginning to face toward Germany and a time when their lives would be uprooted and moved, not to a different town, not to a different location in their country, but to a different nation where God would speak to them in a most marvelous way that would bring change to the world. This bend in the road they were approaching would have a tremendous effect on the spread of the gospel of Jesus Christ in the future.

CHAPTER SEVEN

"THE BOHEMIAN LUTHER"

As Luke of Prague was lying on his deathbed, God was raising up another leader for the Brethren who would lead the Church of the Brethren to newer heights. His name was John Augusta. Augusta was born in 1500 in Prague. He was brought up in the Utraquist Church, and was very faithful to that church for many years. But, something very strange began to happen. He heard from the pulpit of his church, the old Thein Church that the priests of Prague cared for nothing but comfort. Augusta went to other priests and they began to tell him the same story. One day Augusta was riding in a wagon with two priests. One of the priests told Augusta to leave the Utraquist Church and join the Brethren Church. One day Augusta was walking down a road when a priest shouted out to him, "Listen, dear brother! I beseech you. Leave us. You will get no good among us. Go to the Brethren at Bunzlau, and there your soul will find rest." (1)

This absolutely stunned Augusta. For years he had hated the Brethren. He had warned other people against the Brethren. Now he went to the Brethren and found that they were a people who followed the Bible, believed the gospel and enforced their rules without respect to the rank of a person. He didn't know what to do.

He went to his father confessor who told him, "Dear friend, entrust your soul to the Brethren. Never mind if some of them are hypocrites, who do not obey their own rules. It is your business to obey the rules yourself. What more do you want? If you return to us in Prague, you will meet with none but sinners and sodomites." (2)

Augusta joined the Brethren Church. It was not long before the people saw in him the marks of leadership. He was a great preacher, a man who inspired others to follow. He became known as the Bohemian Luther.

At this time there were a group of the younger Brethren who had been to the Wittenberg University and had had many meetings with the students of Martin Luther. They came back to Bohemia teaching that the Brethren Church must move in concerted stride with the Lutheran Church. These younger leaders felt the time had come for the gospel of Jesus Christ to spread in the Protestant movement.

A Synod meeting was called to meet at Brandeis-on-the-Adler. Augusta rose to speak to the assembly. He began to attack the old Executive Council. He said they were guilty of listlessness and sloth, that they did not understand the spirit of the age in which they were living. He ended his talk with the recommendation that he and four other men should be members of the Executive Council. The old men were literally shocked; the young men were thrilled. Augusta was elected and ordained as a Bishop. At the age of 32, Augusta became the leader of the Church of the Brethren. He had three things in his mind that he wanted to accomplish. He wanted friendly relationships with Protestants in other countries. He wanted legal recognition of the Brethren in Bohemia. He wanted union of all Bohemian Protestants.

To accomplish these three goals, the Brethren first is-

sued a new, "Confession of Faith." This confession was presented to Ferdinand, King of Bohemia. They sent this confession to Luther and he praised it. It was read and approved
by John Calvin. The Brethren became widely known across
Europe. Luther had formerly looked up the Brethren as
"sour-looking hypocrites and self-grown saints, who believe
in nothing but what they themselves teach." Now, Luther is
changing his mind. Luther said, "There never have been any
Christians so like the apostles in doctrine and constitution as
these Bohemian Brethren."

At this time, important changes were coming to Bohemia. Bohemia had been at war with the Turks. Louis, King
of Bohemia, fell off his horse while crossing a river, and was
drowned. The old line of Bohemian kings had come to an
end. The crown of Bohemia fell into the hands of the Hapsburgs. The Hapsburgs were staunch supporters of the Roman
Church. Ferdinand I, the new King of Bohemia was also a
brother of the Emperor Charles V, the head of the Holy Roman Empire.

In 1530 Emperor Charles V had threatened to crust
the Reformation by war if necessary. Augusta saw the handwriting on the wall. He knew if the King of Bohemia joined
forces with Emperor Charles V that the days of the Brethren
Church would soon come to an end.

Augusta sent a powerful Baron, Conrad Krajek, a
member of the Brethren Church to speak to King Ferdinand.
He had an audience with the King in Vienna in 1535. The
Baron presented the story of the Brethren to the King. At first
the King was totally opposed to the Brethren, and lost his

temper. Finally, the King told the Baron, "You may believe what you like and we shall not prevent you; but all the same, I give you warning that we shall put a stop to your meetings, where you carry on your hocus-pocus."

The Baron replied, "Your Majesty should not be so hard on me and my noble friends. We are the most loyal subjects in your kingdom." (3)

The interview was over. The Baron left, but three days later two other Barons came and presented to the King the Confession, signed by twelve nobles and thirty-three knights. They said to the King, "Do you really think that it helps the unity of the kingdom when priests are allowed to say in the pulpit that it is less sinful to kill a Picard than it is to kill a dog?"

The King finally promised that as long as the Brethren were loyal to the kingdom he would allow them to worship as they pleased. For a few years all was peaceful. The Brethren began to multiply. Finally they now had four hundred churches and two hundred thousand members in Bohemia.

Augusta made one last trip to Wittenberg to talk to Luther about discipline. He warned Luther that if the German theologians spent their time talking doctrine and did not pay attention to morals, that there would be danger ahead for them. Soon the warning came true.

The Great Reformer of Europe, Martin Luther, died. The Smalkald War broke out and the war spread to Bohemia. Ferdinand, King of Bohemia, gathered his subjects to defend his kingdom and the throne against the Protestant rebels. The Bohemian Brethren were called on to take sides in a civil war. If they fought for Ferdinand, they would be disloyal to their faith. If they fought against Ferdinand, they would be disloyal to their country. The Brethren did the best they could. The Elders issued a prayer to be prayed in all the churches. It was a prayer for the kingdom and the throne.

Then, judgment fell like a mighty hammer. The Battle of Muhlberg was fought on April 24, 1547, and the Protestant troops were soundly defeated. Suddenly the Emperor was the total master of Germany. Ferdinand came back to Prague with vengeance written all over him. He called a council meeting and ordered all papers to be brought to him. He came down on the noblemen and knights with heavy fines and condemned the leaders to death.

On August 22, 1547, four Barons were executed in Prague. The first one to die was Baron Wenzel Petipesky, a member of the Brethren Church. As he was being led to the gallows, he cried out, "My dear Brethren, we go happy in the name of the Lord, for we go in the narrow way." When he reached the place of execution, it was announced that he was dying because he had tried to dethrone King Ferdinand. Petipesky said, "That was never the case." The executioner said, "Never mind, my Lord, it will not help you now." Petipesky replied, "My God, I leave all to Thee." When he said that, his head fell to the ground, separated from his body. (4)

King Ferdinand had heard that John Augusta was the leader of the Brethren. He felt that all the Brethren were traitors to his kingdom. He issued an order that all their meetings were to be cancelled, all their property confiscated, all their churches turned into Roman Catholic Churches, all their priests were to be captured, and that all Brethren who lived on royal estates must either accept the Catholic faith or leave the country within six weeks.

King Ferdinand would never have dreamed what was to happen next.

CHAPTER EIGHT

"THE EXODUS TO POLAND"

When King Ferdinand had issued an order for the Brethren to submit or leave the country within six weeks, he never dreamed they would leave. He thought they would use their sense, abandon their ridiculous religious ways and come back to the bosom of the Roman Catholic Church.

Before the six weeks had gone by, a large number of Brethren said farewell to the only home they had ever known, said good-bye to their familiar hills and valleys and made their way north, over the Giant Mountains to the nation of Poland. It was the month of June. There were about two thousand of them who made this trip. They were protected on the trip by army guards, did not have to pay the toll at the turnpikes, and were supplied with meat, bread, milk and eggs by country peasants.

They marched to Posen where they were greeted and welcomed until the Bishop ordered them to leave. They then marched to Prussia and were ordered away again. They finally found a home in Konigsberg in East Prussia. This was a Lutheran stronghold and the people welcomed them with open arms.

But, it didn't last! They soon learned that the Lutherans could be as bigoted as the Catholics. The Brethren were told they had to accept the Confession of Augsburg if they were to remain there. They could not ordain their own priests. A Brethren priest could not visit a member of his own congregation unless he was accompanied by one of the Lutheran Pastors. They soon discovered that if they were to remain in East Prussia, they would soon cease to be Brethren at all.

In Church History, every time a critical time comes, it seems as if God has a Moses prepared to lead His people out of the wilderness. God had a man prepared in East Prussia. He was George Israel, one of the Brethren. He was a close friend of John Augusta, and gone with him to Wittenberg. Israel was one of the Brethren who had been summoned to Prague to stand before King Ferdinand to answer for his faith and pay a fine of one thousand ducats. He had friends who offered to pay the fine, but George Israel gave them this reply, "No! I have been purchased once and for all with the blood of Christ, and will not consent to be ransomed with the gold and silver of my people. Keep what you have, for you will need it in your flight, and pray for me that I may be steadfast in suffering for Jesus."

George Israel went to Prague, was arrested and thrown into prison. One day, disguised as a clerk, he walked out of the prison and joined the Brethren in Prussia. The Council appointed him as the leader of the exiles.

George Israel knew the gentle Spirit of God had been blowing through Poland. Jerome of Prague had taught in Poland. The people of Poland hated the Roman Church. Many of the young people of Poland had gone to study under Martin Luther. For many years the people had studied the works of Luther and Calvin. So, George Israel left East

Prussia and began a mission tour of Poland. He preached from town to town, most of the time traveling in disguise for the authorities were after him to arrest him. He came to the castle of the Ostrorogs. The Countess warmly welcomed him and Israel was conducting a service in the castle when the Count came home. He heard what was going on, grabbed a whip, and rushed into the room to put a stop to the worship service. When he came into the room, swinging the whip, the preacher, a man named Cerwenka, went on preaching. George Israel said to the Count, "Sir, sit down there!" The Count obeyed, listened and became a convert to Jesus Christ on that very day. He dismissed his Lutheran Chaplain, installed George Israel as his Chaplain and invited the Brethren to come and settle on his huge estate.

The Brethren moved from East Prussia back to Poland to the estate of the Count of Ostrorog. Within seven years the Brethren had founded forty churches in Poland.

As the years went by, the idea began to grow that the Church of the Brethren should be the National Church of Poland. The Lutherans, Zwinglians, Calvinists and Brethren drew closer and closer to one another. Each group wanted to be the national church. Finally, in 1570 the Brethren persuaded all the different groups to father at the United Synod of Sendomir. It was the greatest Synod every held in Poland. It was an attempt to unite all Protestants in Poland to the one grand cause of Jesus Christ. The Calvinists insisted that their confession should be accepted. The Lutherans wanted their Augsburg Confession. Both of these groups turned on the Brethren and accused them of having so many confessions that no one knew which one to accept.

There came a deadlock! The Palatine of Sendomir rose to speak, "For God's sake, for God's sake, remember what depends upon the result of our deliberations, and incline your hearts to that harmony and love which the Lord has commanded us to follow above all things." (1)

When the Palatine of Sendomir finished speaking, he broke into tears. Then the Palatine of Cracow began to sob aloud. They worked out a new confession of faith and all signed it on April 14.

Now, this band of believers who had hammered out their beginning in Bohemia, had been turned out of their own country, made their way to East Prussia and again were rebuffed, now are in Poland to worship God according to their own beliefs. But, their difficulties are not over.

CHAPTER NINE

"MEANWHILE, BACK IN BOHEMIA"

While thousands of the Brethren had fled to Poland, thousands of others had remained in Bohemia. One of those who remained in Bohemia was John Augusta, the Bishop of the Church. King Ferdinand wanted desperately to arrest Augusta. He employed a vicious officer named Sebastian Schoneich to find Augusta and arrest him. Schoneich sent word to Augusta that he wanted to meet with him in the woods to talk. Finally, Augusta agreed, met Schoneich and was arrested.

Augusta was thrown into a dungeon cell and put to the torture. They stripped him naked, stretched him face down on a ladder. They smeared his hips with boiling pitch and then drew the pitch off with tongs with the skin. They hung him from the ceiling by a hook fun through his flesh.

Finally Augusta was transferred to the Castle at Purglitz where for sixteen years Augusta was kept imprisoned. His cell was almost dark. At meals he was permitted to have a candle. He was allowed two rations of meat, two slices of bread, and two jugs of barley beer per day. His shirt was washed every two weeks, his face and hands twice a week, and the rest of his body, never. He was not allowed to speak to the prison guards. He was allowed no paper, no pen, no ink, and no news from the outside world. For three years he sat in darkness, and still he was tortured, but he never denied his Brethren.

Then came an angel to Augusta in the form of a young man who had been brought up among the Brethren. He and his wife lived near the castle and he served as a guard at the prison. Although this young man was a drunkard, he risked his life for Augusta and brought him books, ink, paper, pens, and candles. When Augusta would write something, this young man would see that it got delivered to the Brethren. Augusta would bury all the paper, ink, pens, etc by day, then write at night. From this prison call, Augusta wrote a volume of sermons for the Elders to read. He composed several hymns and wrote the song still sung in the Church:

Praise God forever.

Boundless is his favor,

To his Church and chosen flock,

Founded on Christ the Rock. (1)

Augusta knew that several of the Brethren had fled to Poland. He knew that many, many others had fled to Moravia. Others he knew of who were wandering the countryside as lowly peasants. He also knew there were others who had surrendered and went back to the Church of Rome.

Augusta was the sole surviving Bishop of the Brethren Church. His imprisonment placed the church in a difficult position. Should the Church wait until he was released from prison, or should they select other Bishops? The Church chose to select new Bishops. This offended Augusta. The Church selected Czerny and Cerwenka to the office of Bishop, and then two more Bishops were elected, George Israel and Blahoslaw.

Augusta slowly began to feel that the Church had

ceased to trust him. They did not tell him what they were doing. His authority was gone, his position was lost, and his hopes were dashed. Then, Augusta had something come to his mind. Instead of sulking, he decided to give to the Church his greatest time and skill. He desperately wanted to resume his place in the church and make the Brethren Church the National Church of Bohemia.

Augusta made an appeal to be freed. An avenue of freedom came to him. The official clergy drew up a form of recantation for Augusta to sign. This was his only road to freedom, to recant fully. He must renounce all his religious convictions. He must acknowledge the Roman Catholic Church and submit to this church in all things. He must denounce the Waldenses, Brethren and all other apostates. He must never again interpret the Bible according to his own understanding. He must write out the own recantation in his own handwriting, take a public oath to keep it and have it signed by witnesses.

But, Lord Sternberg came up with another path to freedom. If Augusta could not join the Roman Church, perhaps he could at least join the Utraquists.

John Augusta wrote out his "recantation." He wrote, "I, John Augusta, confess myself a member of the whole Evangelical Church, which, wherever it may be, receives the body and blood of the Lord Jesus Christ in both kinds. I swear that, along with the Holy Catholic Church, I will maintain true submission and obedience to her chief Head, Jesus Christ. I will order my life according to God's holy word and the truth of his pure gospel. I will be led by Him, obey Him

alone, and by no other human thoughts and inventions. I renounce all erroneous and wicked opinions against the holy
universal Christian apostolic faith. I will never take any part
in the meetings of Picards or other heretics." (2)

As the examiners went over his "recantation", they
decided it was no recantation at all. He never mentioned the
Utraquist Church nor the Roman Church. He never made
mention of the Pope.

The authorities refused to release Augusta. Finally
Augusta and his fellow-prisoner, Bilek consented to attend
Mass and have an interview with the Jesuits. At Prague they
were allowed to take a dip in the Royal Bath. It was the first
bath they had had in fourteen years. They were given a bed-
room with good food, wine at dinner and were waited on by
a butler. Finally, the debate with the Jesuits began. He agreed
that the Holy Universal Church was the true bride of Christ.
When it came to the statement that the Holy Christian
Church has never erred and cannot err, Augusta disagreed.
Finally he was sent back to his cell where he languished for
two more years

As early as 1547 Augusta had proposed a National
Protestant Church in Bohemia made up of the Brethren and
the Utraquists. Now he returned to that theme of union with
the Utraquists. Most of the Brethren believed that he was for-
saking the Brethren Church.

Finally, King Maximilian went to the Emperor and
pled for the freedom of Augusta. He was granted freedom
in 1564. His hair was white, his beard was extremely long,
and his health was broken. He spent his last days among the

Brethren, a defeated and broken man. He was restored as an Elder of the Brethren Church, but his influence was gone. He kept pressing his own program of bringing the Brethren and the Utraquists together, but only ended up with having no honor among either church.

Hutton wrote, "As we think of the noble life he lived, and the bitter gall of his eventide, we may liken him to one of those majestic mountains which tower in grandeur under the noontide sun, but round whose brows the vapors gather as night settles down on the earth." (3)

CHAPTER TEN

"THE BRETHREN'S TIME OF PEACE"

The years of 1572-1603 were wonderful years of peace for the Church of the Brethren. It has been called the "Golden Age" for the Brethren.

The Brethren had moved from the strict rules laid down by Peter and Gregory the Patriarch. They now had members out of every rank and class. There were now seventeen barons who were members of the church. In the membership of the church now were knights, capitalists, tradesmen, mayors and generals of the army. One man, Lord High Chamberlain complained that two-thirds of the people of Bohemia were now Brethren.

The Brethren were highly respected in Bohemia. They were industrious and had become prosperous. They were famous for their integrity of character. They built hospitals, and had a fund for those who were poverty-stricken.

In the past the Brethren had shunned education as an evil. Now they had become champions of education to such an extent that they began sending some of their students to foreign universities.

With all of the changes that were happening in the Church, there arose two factions. One faction was led by John Augusta who looked upon the new ways of doing things with horror. He said that all the new idea would bring the Church to absolute ruin. The other faction was led by John Blahoslaw. He had been to Wittenberg and was a master of Greek and Latin. Blahoslaw wrote a scathing paper with John Augusta in mind, "For my part, I have no fear that learned and pious men will ever ruin the Church. I am far more afraid of the action of those high-minded and stupid schemers, who think more highly of themselves than they ought to think. It is absurd to be afraid of learning and culture. As long as our leaders are guided by the Spirit of Christ, all will be well; but when craft and cunning, and worldly prudence creep in, then woe to the Brethren's Church! Let us rather be careful whom we admit to the ministry, and then the Lord will preserve us from destruction." (1)

The faction of Blahoslaw won out. Before long there were forty students in foreign universities, and the Church began to open elementary schools.

In the schools of the Brethren Church, they published a school edition of their Catechism in three languages, Bohemian, German and Latin. So, each student would learn to read from the Catechism, would learn Latin from the Catechism, and learn German from the Catechism. But, all the time the students were learning these languages; they were also learning all the articles of their faith.

In the schools, the Brethren also used a text book called the, "Book of Morals." It was a simple guide to daily living. It was written in rhyme and the children would learn this book, so they could repeat it verbatim.

All this learning, all this memorization, all this repeating the words of the Catechism, where would it lead? The time is coming when the Brethren Church would be crushed to powder. How could they hold on to their faith? How could they stay true to the commands of Christ? It was because they had learned, and hidden in their hearts the words of Scripture in their schools and in their homes.

The Brethren Church was also noted for their deep love of hymns. The Bohemian Brethren were the first to publish a hymnbook. Through the years the leaders of this movement wrote glorious hymns. Among those who wrote hymns were John Hus, John Rockycana, Luke of Prague, Augusta. They were sung to tunes of Gregorian chants and popular melodies of the day. Remember, this was an age when congregational singing was almost unknown. But, the Brethren would all sing together in united praise.

John Blahoslaw, the leader of the progressive movement in the Brethren Church, was an absolute champion of literary work in the Church. He wrote a history of the Brethren. He translated the New Testament into the Bohemian language. He wrote a Bohemian grammar. He wrote a treatise on music.

Times had changed, and the Brethren Church had changed with those times. However, the Church still stood strongly aligned with the fundamentals of the Christian faith. No longer did the Brethren despise education. No longer did they oppose marriage. No longer did they restrict membership in the Church to certain vocations.

It was during this time that a later Catechism was prepared, and the question was asked, "In what way can a sinful man obtain salvation?" The answer that was given, "By the pure grace of God alone, through faith in Jesus Christ our Lord who of God is made unto us wisdom and righteousness and sanctification and redemption." (2)

The Church of the Brethren now seemed to be settled, moving forward in their witness to Bohemia, and at peace. However, dark clouds were looming on the horizon.

CHAPTER ELEVEN

"THE GOLDEN AGE TURNS TO NIGHTMARE"

This period, 1603-1621, sees a drastic turn for the Brethren. The most powerful member of the Brethren Church at this time was Baron Wenzel von Budowa. He was in his fifty's. He was well traveled and influential in the highest courts of Bohemia. He had learned the Turkish and Arabic languages, had studied Islam. He was the recognized leader, not only of the Brethren, but also of all the evangelicals in Bohemia.

The Emperor in Bohemia at this time was Rudolph II. He was a weak man, both in body and in mind. His face was shrunken, his back was bowed, and he tottered when he walked. In 1603, Rudolph did an astounding thing. He revived the Edict of St. James, and ordered all Protestant pastors in the nation to be set aside. He sent a band of armed men to close down the Brethren Churches. He declared that the Church of Rome was the only lawful faith in Bohemia. Diet after Diet was called. At most of these meetings, von Budowa led the way in speaking for the evangelicals of the nation. Finally, Rudolph II issued a notice which read, "No decree of any kind shall be issued either by us or by our heirs and succeeding kings against the above established religious peace." He had recognized the Bohemian National Protestant Confession at last. It seemed as if peace once again was to prevail.

The era of peace turned into a nightmare. When we look at the causes of their ruin, it was not their theology, nor was it their lack of character in living for Jesus Christ. That which brought about their ruin was the fact that they were in the wrong place at the wrong time.

The Church of the Brethren was right in the middle of the politics of Europe. When the Thirty Years' War came, the Brethren found themselves caught in its grip.

There were three things that brought about the nightmare for the Brethren. First, there was the rise of the Jesuits. For several years the Jesuits of the Roman Church had been attacking the Brethren. They had declare, time and again, that the wives of the Brethren ministers were whores, that their children were bastards, that it was better to have the devil visit your house than a Brethren woman.

The second rung in the ladder of the nightmare was the resurgence of the Letter of Majesty. This letter had been ratified by the King and gave the Brethren the right to build churches on royal property. Now the Roman Church began to question this and asked the question, "What is royal property?" Words finally became actions. At Brunau the Roman Abbot turned the Brethren out of their church. At Klostergrab the church was torn down and the wood was used as firewood. The new King, Matthias, took the side of the Catholics. It was finally declared that the Letter of Majesty was invalid because it had been obtained by force and had not been approved by the Pope.

The third rung in the ladder of the nightmare was about the Kingship of Bohemia. Matthias was growing old.

He called a Diet and told the assembled men they were to accept as King his adopted son, Ferdinand Archduke of Styria. The Diet was astounded. They had intended to select a Protestant. Now they were commanded to select the most zealous Catholic in Europe. They bowed to the will of the King and selected Ferdinand as the next King.

Ferdinand was a man of severe piety, a pupil of the Jesuits. He had once said that he had rather beg bread from door to door than allow one single Protestant in his kingdom.

Ferdinand became King. Severe times began for the Protestants of Bohemia. One man, Henry Thurn declared for open rebellion. He advocated dethroning Ferdinand and have his two advisors, Martinic and Slawata, put to death. Thurn gathered a group of men, stormed the royal castle, went into the Regent's Chamber . They threw Martinic, Slawata, and his secretary out the upstairs window, but all three survived the fall.

One can say that this was the beginning of the Thirty Years' War. The Protestant group deposed Ferdinand II, and elected Frederick, son-in-law of James I of England, as King of Bohemia. They ordered all Jesuits out of Bohemia. (1)

We do not know what part the Brethren played in all of this. We do know that the Catholics united against the Protestants. The Catholic army appeared at the walls of Prague and the battle of the White Hill was fought on November 8, 1620. The Protestant Army was defeated; the new King fled from Bohemia, and the nightmare was just beginning.

Prince Lichtenstein was appointed as regent of Prague. He recalled the Jesuits to Bohemia, and ordered all the Brethren to leave the nation.. He put a Roman Catholic priest into every church in Prague, and made an announcement that all the rebels would be freely pardoned and invited all the Protestant nobles to appear before him in Prague. They walked into a trap. When the nobles arrived in Prague, Lichtenstein had forty-seven of them arrested, imprisoned them, and had them tried and convicted. Some were pardoned, but twenty-seven of them were told they would be executed in two days, on June 21st.

The golden age of the Brethren was about to turn into a bloody nightmare.

CHAPTER TWELVE

"THE KILLING BEGINS"

The day of June 21, 1621 will live forever in the memories of the Brethren Church. The City of Prague was divided into two parts, the Old Town and the New Town. The most vivid part of the Old Town was the Great Square. On the west side of the square was the Council House and on the east side of the square was the old, famous Thein Church that had been so important in the history of the Brethren Church.

When dawn broke on the morning of June 21, 1621, the twenty-four prisoners who had been arrested looked out the windows of their prison cells and saw a beautiful, sun-filled day. The church bells chimed the hour of five o'clock in the morning, and a gun was fired at the castle.

It was almost time for the heads of the Bohemian Brethren to fall from the chopping block. It was thought by many to be the closing day of the Bohemian Brethren.

The twenty-four men had spent the night in prayer. Some had taken communion together, while others had spent some time in the singing of Psalms and hymns.

The executioner that day was a man named, Mydlar. He was a Protestant. That day he used four swords for his task and was paid 100 pounds for his gruesome work. With the first sword, he beheaded eleven, with his second sword, five, and with his last two, he beheaded eight men.

When Mydlar flashed his sword into the air and severed the neck of a prisoner, an assistant then placed the dead man's right hand on the block; the sword would then fall again and cut off the right hand. Assistants would then gather up the severed head and hand, wrap them in a black cloth and carry them away.

One of those who were executed that day was Baron Wenzel von Budowa. He had fought so gallantly for the faith. History has recorded for us the last words of Baron Budowa, "My heart impelled me to come to forsake my country and its cause would have been sinning against my conscience. Here am I, my God, do to your servant as seems good to you. I would rather die myself than see my country die." (1)

Two days before the execution, Budowa was visited in prison by two Catholic monks. One of the monks said, "Baron, we wish to show your lordship the way to heaven." The Baron told them he knew the way and was standing on very firm ground.

The monk replied, "My Lord only imagines that he knows the way of salvation. He is mistaken. Not being a member of the Holy Church, he has no share in the Church's salvation." (2)

Budowa told the monk, "I have this excellent promise, whosoever believes in Him shall not perish but have everlasting life. Therefore, until my last moment, will I abide by our true Church."

History tells us that the two monks were horrified. They struck their chests, declared Budowa a heretic, crossed themselves and left him.

The next day two Jesuit priests came to see Budowa. They told him, "We have come to save my lord's soul and to perform a work of mercy."

Budowa said to them, "I thank my God that His Holy Sprit has given me the assurance that I will be saved through the blood of the Lamb. I know whom I have believed; henceforth there is laid up for me a crown of righteousness, which the Lord, the righteous judge, shall give me at that day." (3)

The Jesuits replied to Budowa, "But Paul there speaks of himself, not of others."

Budowa said, "You lie, for does he not expressly add: 'and not to me only, but to all them also that love his appearing." (4) The Jesuits left in disgust

It then came time for Budowa to walk to his place of death. He knelt and prayed. The sword flashed in the sunlight and the "Last of the Bohemians" went home to glory.

When Budowa died, it marked the death of the ancient Church of the Brethren. The death of the Church was only a matter of time.

Following after Budowa was Caspar Kaplit, an old man of eight-six. He wore a white robe to the chopping block. He called it his wedding garment. Then came Otto von Los, who cried out, "Behold I see the heavens opened." Next came Dr. Jessen who had his tongue seized with a pair of tongs, then his tongue was cut off at the roots with a knife, and he died with blood rushing from his mouth.

All these men who died that day were totally committed to Jesus Christ. Their bodies were thrown away and their heads were placed on poles where they remained for ten long years as a warning to everyone who were of the Protestant faith.

Ferdinand was absolutely determined to crush the Church of the Brethren. His aim was to wipe their memory from the face of Bohemia. He turned every Brethren Church into a Roman Catholic Church. Priests came into these churches, lashed the pulpits with whips, beat all the altars with sticks, sprinkled holy water through-out the buildings to cleanse them from the Brethren curse.

While all of this was going on, the Brethren were being expelled from Bohemia. Thirty-six thousand Brethren families left Bohemia and Moravia. The population of Bohemia went from three million to one million. The property was given over to the King, and the University of Prague was handed over to the Jesuits. The Bibles, hymnals, confessions, and catechisms of the Brethren Church were burned by the thousands upon thousands. For six long, torturous years the nation of Bohemia was a big field of blood. Brethren were chopped to pieces, burned alive, and hanged from every tree and post that could be found.

Hutton wrote in his book, "The Ancient Church of the Bohemian Brethren bade a sad farewell to the land of its birth, and disappeared from the eyes of mankind."

From all outward appearances, the Church of the Brethren was dead and gone from Bohemia. It took Ferdinand six years to accomplish this. However, in spite of all the killing, all the cruelty, all the banishment of the Brethren from Bohemia and Moravia, there were thousands of people who remained Brethren in their hearts. In 1781, when Joseph II issued the Edict of Toleration, 100,000 people in Bohemia and Moravia declared themselves to be Brethren.

Word was sent to the Pope in Rome that the Church of the Brethren no longer existed, but the Lord God knew better. For five generations the faith of the Brethren was handed down in secret from father to son, and the Church continued to live.

CHAPTER THIRTEEN

"THE CHURCH IN HIDING"

The year of 1621 became the year of blood. It was absolute slaughter for the members of the Brethren Church. After the slaughter had taken place, thousands upon thousands of Brethren were rounded up and forced to leave Bohemia and Moravia. King Ferdinand was so confident that he sent word to the Pope in Rome that the Church of the Brethren no longer existed.

However, God had something else in mind. God always has a people. God can always bring to light his purpose through the lives of people who truly love Him.

The purpose and plan of God was brought to light in the life of a man named John Amos Comenius. Comenius was born in 1592 in a little town in Moravia. When he was six years of age, both of his parents died. He was raised by a sister and educated in one of the Brethren schools. He felt that God wanted him to be a minister. He went to the Calvinist University of Herborn, then to the Calvinist University of Heidelberg. He became minister of the church at Fulneck. Then, Comenius was married and had children, and felt contented and happy. But this happiness soon turned to much sorrow when the Thirty Years' War started.

Comenius was serving as Pastor of the Church in Fulneck, happy, joyful, full of life with his dear wife and children. Suddenly, the troops of Ferdinand entered Fulneck and began killing, hacking, torturing, burning and hanging people. Comenius wrote in one of his books, "Almighty God, what is happening? Must the whole world perish?"

Comenius escaped Fulneck with his family, and made his way to a nearby estate where Gregory the Patriarch had lived, and was buried. On the way, Comenius lost his wife and one of his children. He began writing about the times in which he was living, all the horrible sights he had seen. During this time he wrote his beautiful allegory, "The Labyrinth of the World and the Paradise of the Heart." (1)

With all the evil that Comenius had seen, he reached the conclusion that the only answer to all of this was the wonderful, beautiful faith of the Church of the Brethren. In 1628 Comenius left the estate, Brandeis-on-the-Adler. The Baron of this estate had been allowed to give shelter to forty ministers, but now the order had come that all the ministers had to leave. This band of exiles, ministers of the Brethren Church, left and made their way to Poland. The leader of this group was Comenius. As the group reached a certain point on the Giant Mountains, they looked back and Comenius prayed that in their old home God would preserve a "Hidden Seed" which would one day grow into a tree. This group of ministers turned and began marching down the mountain toward Poland. As they marched, they were singing a song,

Naught have we taken with us,
All to destruction is hurled,
We have only our Kralitz Bibles,
And our Labyrinth of the World.

We do not know what happened to many of the exiles. We do know that some of the Brethren went to Hungary, some made their way to Saxony and became Lutherans, others made their way to Holland and became Reformed Protestants, while still others crossed the sea and made their way to England. But, the ones who will prove to be so important in our story became known as the "Hidden Seed." This "Hidden Seed" buried their Bibles in their gardens, tucked their records away in the thatched roofs of their homes, made concentrated efforts to memorize the Book of Revelation, and waited for the time when the call would come from God for them to arise in the power of the Holy Spirit once again.

After the slaughters of 1621, and the expulsion of the Brethren from Bohemia and Moravia, John Comenius never gave up hope that the Brethren Church would rise again. He accepted the position as teacher in the school at Lissa with one goal in mind; to revive the Church of the Brethren. Everything he taught, everything he did was pointed to one simple goal. He encouraged all the homes to teach the children the pure, unadulterated Word of God in the home. He asked the parents to discipline the children to the ancient teachings of the Brethren. He believed that if the children would grow up with this type of teaching, they would bring about the revival of the Brethren Church.

Comenius wrote a book, "School of Infancy." He firmly believed that the only sure foundation for the teaching of children was to be done by the mother in the home in the first six years of the child's life. In this book he wrote, Comenius taught that the mother's life must be of a certain kind even before the birth of the child. He taught that the expectant mother must be cheerful, moderate in her diet, avoid all worry, and keep in touch with God through prayer. The mother must nurse the child, and when weaned, feed the child plain food. The mother must teach the child to be clean in habits, to obey his superiors, to be truthful and polite, to kneel in prayer, and to remember that the God revealed in Jesus Christ was close at hand at all times. (2)

As the Thirty Years War began to draw to a close, Comenius look forward to the day when the Brethren Church would be able to return to Bohemia and Moravia, but the Peace of Westphalia broke his heart. In this document, no provision was made at all for the Brethren to return home. Comenius became very disheartened. However, the more man disappointed him, the more he believed that God would take up the cause of the Brethren. He wrote a letter in which he said, "If there is no help from man, there will be from God, whose aid is wont to commence when that of man ceases."

The Brethren faithfully held on in Lissa, but as Comenius tried to revive the church and its schools, suddenly horrible war broke out. Charles X became the King of Sweden. John Casimir, the King of Poland, made a claim to the throne of Sweden. The two kings went to war. Charles X, who was a Protestant invaded Poland and captured the town of Lissa. In 1656 the Polish army surrounded the city of Lissa. The Swedish army gave way and the Polish army gained control of the city. The library of Comenius was burned and his school was turned to ashes. The whole town of Lissa was set to the torch. The Brethren fled the city of Lissa in wagons and on foot. The Polish army chased the Brethren across the countryside.

One of the stories that has come down to us of this pursuit was that of Samuel Kardus. Samuel was caught; his head was placed between a door and the doorpost. As the door was slowly closed, his head was slowly crushed into pieces.

By this time, John Comenius was getting very old. He had seen all of his hopes and dreams dashed to pieces. His Church was scattered across the countryside like leaves in the wind.

In the middle of all this suffering, an invitation came from Oliver Cromwell of England. He offered to bring the Brethren to Ireland and give them a home. Comenius refused. For some reason Comenius fell under the influence of a man named Drabik. He was a rank impostor who said he had had a revelation from heaven. He said that in this vision he saw that the Brethren would be allowed to return to their homeland, so Comenius chose to believe this, turned down the invitation for his people to go to Ireland and waited, in vain, for the return of the Church to Bohemia and Moravia.

Comenius was the link between the old Church of the Brethren and the renewed Church of the Brethren. He ordained his son-in-law, Peter Jablonsky, then Peter ordained his own son, Daniel Ernest, then Daniel ordained David Nitschmann. This David Nitschmann became the first Bishop of the Renewed Church of the Brethren.

This "Hidden Seed", those who were worshipping in secret in Bohemia and in Moravia, kept on seeking the Lord, kept on studying the Word of God, kept on praying, kept on training their children in the way of God.

John Comenius died in 1672, and it would be fifty

more years before the "Hidden Seed" would come out into the light of freedom in their worship of God.

CHAPTER FOURTEEN

"GERMAN PIETISM"

The pressure of persecution became so heavy that one group of families decided they would leave Bohemia and the district of Moravia and head for a part of Germany where they knew there were Christians who would be sympathetic to their way of worship. They found such a group in Germany known as the German Pietists.

German pietism had grown out of the Lutheran Church of the late 1600's because the Lutheran Church had become so cold, dead, hard and dry as a pile of bones. They sought to raise the spiritual temperature of the people of God. They had no interest in leaving the Lutheran Church, but were interested in raising the level of piety and practice in the church. They did not want to start another denomination. George Henry Overton, the Methodist scholar, said, "They aimed chiefly at throwing some life into the dry bones of prevailing orthodoxy."

That is exactly what God does in times of revival. He throws spiritual life into the dry bones of prevailing orthodoxy. The man who began pietism was Phillip Spener. He had studied in Switzerland, Germany and France. He finally settled down and became a Pastor of a Lutheran Church in Frankfort, Germany. While Pastor of that church, he began to hold house meetings and fellowship groups in his own home for the revitalization of dead orthodoxy. These meetings were prayer groups and Bible study groups. He sometimes would

hold question and answer sessions. These house groups began to multiply. They became known as the School of Piety.
Spener published a little book called, "Pietist Desires." It was
a book of doctrine and practical helps. When people in the
groups would began to take this little book seriously, then
they would become leaders in other groups.

Another man who was instrumental in the German
Pietist movement was Augustus Frank. He was a professor at
Leipzig University. He was Phillip Spener's advisor and sup-
porter. Frank established a Pietistic Center and the teaching
of the Bible began to flourish. The house groups began studying the Bible in the original languages. Their primary aim as
they studied the Bible was to answer the question, "How does
the Scripture apply to me? What is God saying to me?"

The Pietist movement began to grow, with Spener
as its pastoral leader and Frank as it scholarly leader. Then,
along came a man named Gerhart and he began to turn this
teaching to song. The hymns Gerhart wrote are dominated
by a passionate devotion to Jesus Christ, and great confidence in the love of God. One hymn Gerhart wrote speaks:

My Savior, how shall I proclaim it?
How pay the mighty debt I owe,
Let all I have, and all I am
Ceaseless to all Thy glory show.

To much to Thee I cannot give,
To much I cannot do for Thee,
Let all Thy love, and all Thy grief,
Graven on my heart shall ever be. (1)

German Pietism, which began as a small stream, became a flowing river, then a mighty torrent, flooding across Europe.

The Pietists wrote down a list of things that were of deep concern to them in the church of their day. Look at this list!

A recognition that all is not well with institutional Christianity. The need for a renewal of the original spirit of the gospel in terms of a personal experience with Christ, and not formal adherence to a church.

The need for warm, evangelical preaching.

The need for small groups to come together in order that spiritual life might be cultivated and seen to grow.

The desperate need for an injection of realism and fervency in the praise of God.

Educational projects and missionary involvement that shows that this pietism does not remain in the heart, but moves out to change the world. (2)

Isn't that what we need today in the church? We look out today at a dry, brittle church in America and know that something must happen for us to come back to true, vital Christianity. That something is revival! There is so much dryness today. Every person reading this book knows that we need a fresh infilling of the Holy Spirit in our lives.

It was into this type of atmosphere that a small group of Moravians would come. Undoubtedly, they would be influenced, in some measure, by German Pietism.

CHAPTER FIFTEEN

"ENTER: COUNT ZINZENDORF"

We have walked through the centuries, looking at men who were leaders in a movement to bring back New Testament Christianity. We have looked at the Bohemian Brethren, the Unitas Fratrum or Unity of the Brethren, the Church of the Brethren, the Hidden Seed, and now we will look at this group who has been banished from their homeland, looking for a place where they would be free to worship according to their own hearts. This group became known as the Moravians.

The Moravian Church today is a small group in our world. There are today about one million members worldwide. There is a group of Moravians in a settlement outside Leeds, England, but the largest group of Moravians today is in Tanzania in Africa.

The Moravian revival which has come to be called the "Moravian Pentecost" was a one-day event that reverberated across the years, and had a tremendous impact on Christianity in many different parts of the world. This one-day Pentecost took place on August 13, 1727 in the little village of Herrnhut, Germany.

About ten miles from the southern border of Saxony, Germany stands the ruins of the Castle Gross-Hennersdorf. This border joins the country of Bohemia. It was in this castle that Ludwig Zinzendorf, who became the main instrument in the renewal of the Brethren Church, spent his childhood.

Zinzendorf was born on May 26, 1700 in Dresden. Today one can view the house in which he was born. The street on which this house sits is now named, "Zinzendorf Street." His father died when he was only six weeks old. He was four years of age when his mother married again, and the young count was given over to his grandmother, Catherine von Gersdorf, to raise in the Gross-Hennersdorf Castle. His grandmother called him, "little Lutz."

The childhood of Zinzendorf was remarkable. It is strange how God seems to pick out a person to do great work for Him.

Zinzendorf read the Bible every day. He memorized Luther's Catechism. His Aunt Henrietta prayed with him every morning and evening. Zinzendorf said, "At the age of four I loved the Savior, and had abundant communion with Him. In my fourth year I began to seek God earnestly, and determined to become a true servant of Jesus Christ."(1) It was at the age of four that Zinzendorf composed his personal covenant. He wrote, "Dear Savior, do Thou be mine, and I will be Thine." Zinzendorf walked through his life with a single motto, "I have one passion. It is Jesus, Jesus only."

As a young child, Zinzendorf walked with the Lord. He once said, "I heard Him speak in my heart, and saw Him with the eye of faith." It seemed that the blessed fire of the Holy Spirit burned in his heart from an early age. He once wrote, concerning these early years, "Of all the qualities of Christ, the greatest is His nobility; and of all the noble ideas in the world, the noblest is the idea that the Creator should die for His children. If the Lord were forsaken by all the world, I still would cling to Him and love Him."

However, a cruel period began in his life at the age of ten. His mother enrolled him in a school at Halle. In this school he was ridiculed because of his nobility, he was beaten by his teachers, and treated as a liar and an idiot. At this time in his life, Zinzendorf was quite weak and suffered from a constant cough. He was bullied unmercifully in the school. At this school, half treated him as a rogue and the other half treated him as an idiot. On one occasion he was made to stand in the street with a pair of donkey's ears on his head and a sign on his back reading, "lazy donkey."

In spite of all that was happening to him in school, Zinzendorf learned Greek and Latin, and learned to speak French. As he grew, he became bolder and stood his ground with the bullies in the school. At last he gathered around him five boys with whom he formed a group they called the "The Slaves of Virtue." They later changed the name of this club, "The Honorable Order of the Mustard Seed." (2) They pledged themselves to be true to Jesus Christ. As this club grew, other boys would join. Among this group of boys were John Potter, who became the Archbishop of Canterbury; Thomas Wilson, Bishop of Sodor; Cardinal Noailles; and General Oglethorpe, who became Governor of Georgia.

Zinzendorf's uncle became quite concerned that his nephew was becoming too religious. His station in life was to serve the state. His father had been Secretary of State and "little Lutz" was to follow in his footsteps. His uncle had a deep contempt for the Pietist religion, and sent Zinzendorf to the University of Wittenberg, "to drive the nonsense out of him."

At the University of Wittenberg, Zinzendorf hit upon the idea that the teachings of the Lutherans and the Pietists could be reconciled. He began talking to his professors about this and some of them began to agree with him. When Zinzendorf's mother heard of this, she wrote to him, "You must not meddle in such weighty matters; they are above your understanding and your powers." (3) Zinzendorf obeyed his mother, because he was following the fourth commandment.

After his education at Wittenberg, he followed the usual pattern of nobility by being sent on a grand tour. He looked upon this tour with absolute horror. He did not want to go, for he thought he would see things that would distract him from his love of Christ.

On this grand tour, Zinzendorf visited Frankfurt, Dusseldorf, Brussels, Antwerp, Amsterdam, Rotterdam, and ended with a six month stay in Paris.

On this tour, while in Dusseldorf, an important event happened that had a profound effect on Zinzendorf's life. He was in a picture gallery looking at the beautiful "Ecce Homo" of Domenico Feti. At the bottom of the picture, he read the words, "All this I did for thee; what doest thou for Me?" Standing at this picture, Zinzendorf vowed to live for Christ who had worn the crown of thorns for everyone.

When this grand tour was completed, Zinzendorf went home. He was now twenty years old. He stopped to visit his aunt, the Countess of Castell and her daughter Theodora. While visiting them, he fell ill with a fever and had to stay much longer than he had planned. As the time passed, he found that he was in love with his young cousin, Theodora. He became so thrilled to know that he would have such a sweet mate. He paid a visit to his friend Count Beuss and, as they talked, he discovered that Count Beuss also wished to marry Theodora. Each one of the men volunteered to step aside for the other, but they soon decided to go to Theodora and let her make the decision. Theodora pledged her love to Count Reuss.

Eighteen months later, on September 7, 1722, at the age of 22, Zinzendorf married Count Reuss's sister, Erdmuth Dorothea. Truly God had watched out after his child, for in later years, the people of Herrnhut called her a princess of God and the "foster-mother of the Brethren's Church." (4)

Zinzendorf had a strong desire to enter the ministry of the Lutheran Church, but, in that day and time, it was considered beneath the dignity of a nobleman to be a minister. He accepted a position as the King's Councilor in Dresden. He decided if he could not be a pulpit preacher, he could teach in other ways. He began to invite people to his home to weekly meetings on Sunday afternoon from three until seven. At these meetings, a passage of Scripture would be read, then all present would discuss the Scripture and talk about spiritual things.

However, Zinzendorf was not content. He reasoned in his mind that if Christian fellowship was good for the lords and ladies, it would also be good for the poor people. He bought from his grandmother the estate of Berthelsdorf in 1722. He installed his friend, John Andrew Rothe, as Pastor of the village church. Zinzendorf said, "I bought this estate because I wanted to spend my life among peasants and win their souls for Christ."

Zinzendorf was a loyal member of the Lutheran Church, he knew Luther's theology by heart, and now he was making an effort to carry out the dreams of Luther to take the gospel of Christ to the people.

Zinzendorf introduced the new pastor to the people of the village of Berthelsdorf. The induction sermon was preached by Schafer, the Pietist pastor at Gorlitz. No greater words of prophecy could be uttered than words Schafer said in his sermon, "God will light a candle on these hills which will illuminate the whole land." Those words came true five years later.

One day Zinzendorf went to the public library in Dresden. He found a book which utterly amazed him. It was the story of the Moravian Christians, going all the way back to the time of John Huss. This was like a bolt of lightning to him. At first he thought the Moravians were a small sect that needed to be brought under the umbrella of the Lutheran Church, but he found that this group could trace their roots farther back than Martin Luther. Zinzendorf had found a remnant of the church that was older than his own.

CHAPTER SIXTEEN

"FROM SHEPHERD BOY TO SERVANT OF THE LORD"

Across Christian centuries, it has been a well-founded belief that every believer stands on the same level before God. No one believer in Jesus Christ is more important in the Kingdom of God than another. However, often there comes into the work of God on this earth a man or woman who stands out, who stands totally committed to the Lord Jesus Christ and God uses that individual in a wonderful, marvelous way. Such was a man named Christian David, a shepherd boy who became a servant of the Lord.

Christian David was born in 1680 in Senftleben, Moravia. His family was devout Roman Catholic. While growing up, this young man worked as a shepherd boy out in the pastures, was faithful at Catholic Mass. He was completely devoted to his patron Saint Anthony, and was always careful to kneel before every image or picture of the Virgin Mary. As he roamed the pastures with herds of sheep, his mind grew quite anxious with the passing years. For all his faithfulness to his church, for all his devotion to the Virgin Mary, he was never sure how he stood with God. No one is sure why, but he went to a small group of Protestants for advice, and, to his horror, they told him the Pope was the Anti-Christ, that the worship of saints was wrong. The thing that stuck with him was, they told him that only faith in Jesus

Christ would forgive his sins.

Christian David watched these Protestant men. When some of them were arrested and thrown into prison, Christian David stood outside the jail and listened to them singing praises to God in their cells. He began to read Lutheran books that condemned the Pope, and Papal books that condemned the Lutherans. He became quite unhappy with both of them. As time went on, Christian David became so confused that he began to hate the name of Christ.

In his unhappiness, Christian David went to some Jews and began to study with them. They agreed with his doubts concerning the New Testament and told him only the Jews were the true Israel of God.

At the age of 20, Christian David returned to the Bible. He read the Old Testament, then the New Testament. He reached a deep conviction that Jesus Christ was the Messiah that was promised, and that the Bible was the Word of God.

There was still a restlessness in Christian David. He could not find peace in his soul. He left Moravia, traveled through Hungary and finally made his way to Berlin, Germany. In Berlin, he joined a Lutheran Church, but found that church so cold in spirit. He left Berlin and joined the Prussian Army. In 1717, at the age of 27, Christian David left the army and made his way to Gorlitz, Silesia. He came into contact with two preachers of the Pietist movement, Schafer and Schwedler. He found in these two men something for which he had been looking for a long, long time. Suddenly, Christian David fell ill. He was bedfast for twenty weeks, but Schwedler visited him every day. Through the ministry and counsel of this dear man, Christian David at last found peace with Jesus Christ. He came to the strong conviction that he had been forgiven of his sins. Christian David married a member of Schwedler's church, and joined the church himself.

For the next five years, Christian David made his home in Gorlitz. He made a few trips back to Moravia, at the risk of his own life. There he would tell people of the new joy he had found in Jesus Christ. He became known in Moravia as the "Bush Preacher."

For 340 years there had been a neighborhood of Germans in Fulneck, Moravia. They spoke the German language, had German names, a German Bible, and sang German hymns. Some of these German families were the Schneiders, the Nitschmann, the Stachs, the Zeisbergers, the Jaeschkes, the Neissers, and, in Christian David's old home, the Grassmanns. They knew no peace. Some were thrown into prison, some were chained, others were yoked to a plow. The old patriarch of the Germans, George Jaeschke, was on his deathbed, he gathered his son and grandsons around him and spoke to them in prophetic words of a remnant that would be saved. He told them, "It is true that our liberties are gone, and that our descendants are giving way to a worldly spirit, so that the Papacy is devouring them. It may seem as though the final end of the Brethren's Church had come. But, my beloved children, you will see a great deliverance. The remnant will be saved. How, I cannot say; but something tells me that an exodus will take place, and that a refuge will be offered in a country and on a spot where you will be able, without fear, to serve the Lord according to His holy Word."

When Christian David heard of the sufferings of these Germans, he resolved in his heart to rescue them. Schafer had introduced him to Rothe; Rothe introduced him to Zinzendorf. Christian David asked Zinzendorf for permission to bring persecuted Protestants from Moravia to the refuge of Berthelsdorf. Zinzendorf told David that if they came, they would find a place to live.

At 10:00 at night, on May 27, 1722, Christian David met with a small group in the home of Jacob Neisser. (1) The small group consisted of Augustin and Jacob Neisser, their wives and children, Martha Neisser, and Michael Jaeschke. We know so little about these dear people. We do not know if they were descendants of the Church of the Brethren, but they made their way across the mountains. They left all of their belongings behind. On June 8, 1722, this small band of believers in Jesus Christ arrived at Count Zinzendorf's estate with Christian David, the shepherd boy who became a servant of the Lord, leading them.

CHAPTER SEVENTEEN

"DESTINATION: HERRNHUT"

When John Wesley visited Herrnhut, he wrote in his journal that he heard Christian David preach, and that he was a great preacher.

Today, if you were to visit Herrnhut, you would find a quiet, very neat village with well-kept houses. There is the Brethren's House, which is the place where unmarried members of the village live, the Sister's House, where unmarried women lived. There was never any suggestion that these dear unmarried people lived as monks or nuns. They were completely free to live in these large houses if they so chose, or they could leave anytime these would wish to do so. If you visited Herrnhut, you would also find the Manor House, which is the repository of all the archives of the Moravians. You would find hundreds of manuscripts, eight thousand biographies of Moravian members who have died. There is also a manuscript in John Huss's own handwriting. This manuscript is over 600 years old. You would also find a Hebrew Bible, which once belonged to Martin Luther, which Count Zinzendorf acquired at Wittenberg. (1)

If you visited Herrnhut today, you could walk along a tree-shaded street to the Moravian cemetery. Over the entrance is written the inscription, "Jesus is risen from the dead." On the inside is the inscription, "He is become the first fruits of them that sleep." Just inside the gate to the cemetery, on the left, is the grave of Christian David. All the gravestones face the east, waiting for the day of resurrection. Only names and dates are recorded on the gravestones.

However, when Christian David and his small bank of refugees from Moravia arrived in 1722, there was no Herrnhut.

When Christian David and the others arrived at the estate of Count Zinzendorf, Zinzendorf was away on a trip. The manager (steward) of his estate, a man named Heitz, was in charge of his affairs. Heitz thought it best that the Moravians should be settled at a safe distance from the village of Berthelsdorf in case there was any disease among the new settlers. He led the Moravians to a piece of ground about one mile from Berthelsdorf, a piece of ground that was swampy, empty, quite dismal. The only improvement on the ground was an old unfinished farmhouse. This piece of ground was at the top of a sloping hill, and had become known as Hutberg, which means Watch-Hill. It was a place that had often been used as camping ground by gypsies, or other traveling salesmen. The road was so bad that wagons would sometimes sink into the mud up to the axles.

Heitz, the manager of Zinzendorf's estate, became very concerned about the welfare of the refugees. He found a spring which would provide water for them, and over that spot he offered a prayer, "Upon this spot, in Thy name, I will build for them the first house." Heitz began to spread the word concerning the newly arrived settlers. Lady Gersdorf gave them a cow. Heitz and Christian David walked over the area, marking trees that could be cut down. They began to cut trees and build houses. At first, the Moravians were in despair. The food was very poor, many of them became sick, the people in the area laughed at them, and when they built the first house, the people of the area said it would fall down soon.

Christian David was not disheartened. He could see in his mind a good village. He mapped out, in his mind, the streets of the town, and shared his dreams with Heitz. Heitz wrote a letter to Zinzendorf, "God grant that your Excellency may be able to build on the hill the, Hutberg, a town which may not only itself abide under the Lord's Watch (Herrnhut), but all the inhabitants of which may also continue on the Lord's Watch, so that no silence may be there by day or night." Because of this letter, the new village received its name, Herrnhut, which means, "The Lord's Watch."

When Zinzendorf returned, he was driving along the road, saw a light in the trees and asked what the light was. He was told it was the light of the first house the Moravians had built. He stopped his carriage, went into the house and assured the people in the house of his goodwill. He went down on his knees and commended these dear people to the care of Almighty God.

But, something was gnawing at the heart of Christian David. His wife went through a very dangerous illness. He promised God that if she survived, he would answer the gnawing in his heart, return to Moravia, and seek other persecuted believers. He was working in the fields. Suddenly, he threw down his tools, left in his working clothes, and made his way to Sehlen, the old home of the Neissers. He begged the rest of the family to cross into Germany with him. After a few days, a small band of eighteen people made their way to Herrnhut with Christian David.

Christian David went back to find more people. At this time in his life, Christian David knew very little of the old Church of the Brethren. But, in Zauchtenthal, he found five young men who were a part of the old ancient church. They were David Nitschmann I, David Nitschmann II, David Nitschmann III, Melchior Zeisberger, and John Toeltschig. David the II was the first Bishop of the Renewed Church of the Brethren. Melchior Zeisberger was the father of the apostle to the Indians. John Toelschig was the first Moravian preacher in Yorkshire. While Christian David was searching for others to come to Herrnhut, these five young men had come to a crisis time in their lives. They were ordered to appear before the judge, who happened to be Toeltschig's father. He ordered them to cease their meetings. They decided to leave and make their way to Lissa in Poland where there were other Brethren. As they made their way to Lissa, they sang an old Moravian song as they traveled:

Blessed be the day when I must roam,
Far from my country, friends and home,
An exile poor and mean;
My father's God will be my guide,
Will angel guards for me provide?
My soul in dangers screen.
Himself will lead me to a spot
Where, all my cares and griefs forgot,
I shall enjoy sweet rest.
As pants for cooling streams the hart,

I languish for my heavenly part,
For God, my refuge blest.

These five young men had heard of Christian David, and of the beginning settlement at Herrnhut. They decided to pay a visit to Herrnhut on their way to Lissa. They arrived in Herrnhut on May 12, 1724. They had thought they would find a thriving town, but all they found were three small houses.

These five young men watched. They saw Christian David working on another building. In the afternoon, Count Zinzendorf and his wife appeared. The Count laid the foundation stone for a college. They heard the Count deliver a speech, and de Watteville offering a prayer. They were touched in their heart, and decided to stay.

Christian David returned again and again to the old country. He made ten trips back, finding more believers to bring to Herrnhut. He found some who were in prison, living in filthy cells, others who were living under hedges, and others who had been beaten. All of these were sons and daughters of well-to-do people. They all made their way to Herrnhut with Christian David and made their home among other believers who were free to worship God. The village of Herrnhut reached a population of about 600 people during these days.

None of us will ever know the debt we owe to Christian David. As you trace Christian history from Christian David, to Peter Bohler (more on Bohler later), to John Wesley, to revival in America, you will find that we have had the opportunity to know Jesus Christ as Savior and Lord because of this one man who, through grit, determination, and the leadership of the Holy Spirit, made a path for us to come to Christ.

CHAPTER EIGHTEEN

"SATAN ARRIVES IN HERRNHUT"

One day Zinzendorf was in the public library in Dresden. He found a book, which utterly amazed him. It was the story of these Moravian Christians, going all the way back to the time of John Huss. This struck Zinzendorf like a bolt of lightning. He had believed that the Moravians were a small sect and needed to be brought under the umbrella of the Lutheran Church. Now, he had found that this group could trace their roots farther back than Martin Luther. Here was a remnant of the church older than his own. In a sense, Zinzendorf left the settlers in Herrnhut much to themselves from 1722 to 1727.

Without warning, serious divisions began to arise among the Moravians. Many of those who had come to this new settlement had not belonged to the original Hidden Seed. Only five of them could trace themselves back to the original group. All the rest of the inhabitants of Herrnhut were people of different stripes: some were Catholics, some Lutherans, some Separatists, some did not believe in the Holy Trinity, some were Calvinists, some were evangelicals from Swabia, some spent their time arguing free-will and predestination. The result was serious division in the town. As the settlers of Herrnhut got to know each other better, they began to love each other less and less. As they loved each other less, severe theological dispute ran rampant through the small town.

Then, a man arrived in Herrnhut who became the capstone of discord. His name was Kruger. He had come from Ebersdorf where he had been kicked out of the Lutheran Church. He came to Herrnhut and began to preach against the Lutheran Church. The more he preached, the more people looked on him as a saint. He told the people that he had been called by God to reform Count Zinzendorf. He referred to Rothe as the "False Prophet", and Zinzendorf as "The Beast." He called the Lutheran Church "Babylon", and told all the people of Herrnhut to leave that church. (1)

The word, "kruger", in Low German means "tavern-keeper", and in High German means, "potter." This man, Kruger became highly successful in Herrnhut. Many of the people of Herrnhut became convinced that the Lutheran Church was a den of thieves and stopped attending the parish church in Brethelsdorf. Even Christian David was led astray by this man. David even built a new house away from the people so his life would not be tainted by the teachings of the Lutherans.

Finally Kruger went out of his mind and was committed to an insane asylum in Berlin. It seemed that the whole town of Herrnhut was now filled with religious fanatics.

Now came the time for Count Zinzendorf to step in and do something. Basically, he had left the Moravians alone for the past four or five years. Zinzendorf had been very busy. He had official state business to conduct. He tried his best to spend the wintertime in the city, but spent summers in the country close to Herrnhut. When the village of Herrnhut had first started, Zinzendorf had made two important rules they were to follow. Rule #1 stated that no refugee could settle in Herrnhut who was not forced to do so except by persecution. Rule #2 stated that all of the settlers in Herrnhut had to promise that they would remain faithful to the Augsburg Confession, which is the official confession of the Lutheran Church.

While things were getting worse and worse in Herrnhut, things were getting better and better in the near-by village of Brethelsdorf. Zinzendorf had started a school for the sons of noblemen in Herrnhut and a school for the daughters of noblemen in the village of Brethelsdorf. The estate manager, Heitz, was busy teaching Bible lessons. Pastor Rothe of the Brethelsdorf Church was preaching sermons on spiritual awakening. The village of Brethelsdorf was spiritually stirred, the church was crowded.

Zinzendorf could tell that things in Herrnhut were getting worse and worse. He knew he was going to have to take serious measures. Christian David had called Pastor Rothe a narrow-minded churchman. Rothe had called the people of Herrnhut "mad fanatics" from the pulpit. Matters had reached a critical stage.

The spiritual tide had gone out at Herrnhut. There is nothing attractive about the tide being out. There is no beautiful water moving, swelling, lapping against the shore. No fish are darting in the water. No swimmers are running along the shore laughing and playing. The tide is out.

The tide had gone out in Herrnhut. That which these dear refugees had longed for had eroded. Bickering and resentment had become the rule of the day.

BUT, the tide is about to roll in. There is nothing as beautiful as when the tide comes in. Once again, people are laughing and playing. Joy becomes the rule of the day. That is about to happen at Herrnhut.

Following Pages:
The Original Moravian Founders and Leaders

Count Zinzendorf

John Cennick

Anna Nitschmann

Peter Bohler

David Zeisberger

David Nitschmann

Leonard Doeber

Christian David

Grave of Christian David

Ancient Herrnhut

John Wesley

Comenius

John Huss

CHAPTER NINETEEN

"PENTECOST COMES TO HERRNHUT"

When true, authentic revival comes, it seems unreal, something totally out of this world. When revival came to the village of Herrnhut, it seemed like that to the refugees from Moravia.

When Zinzendorf became aware of the dissension and quarreling among the people of Herrnhut, he immediately became more involved with them. He did not turn his back on any of them. Zinzendorf said of Christian David, "Although our dear Christian David was calling me the Beast and Mr. Rothe the False Prophet, we could see his honest heart nevertheless, and knew we could lead him right. It is not a bad maxim when honest men are going wrong to put them into office, and they will learn from experience what they will never learn from speculation."

Zinzendorf gathered all of the villagers to a mass meeting in the Great House in Herrnhut. He spoke to them for over three hours on the sin of division. He read to them the "Manorial Injunctions and Prohibitions", which all the villagers had to promise to obey. These injunctions and prohibitions are today known as "The Brotherly Agreement of the Moravian Church." This agreement is divided into six sections:

The ground of our witness

The witness of the Christian life

The witness of the living church
The witness of the Christian home
The witness of a Christian citizen
Our witness to the world (1)

Zinzendorf read all of this to the village of Herrn-hut on May 12, 1727. It might be proper to ask the question, "What kind of man was this Count Zinzendorf that he could exercise such power over this group of Moravian refugees?" Zinzendorf was 27 years of age at this time, about the average age of the inhabitants of Herrnhut. He remembered the time, as a child, when Phillip Spener, the father of the German Pietists, told him of the two missionaries who had gone out to South India. Zinzendorf later wrote, "There and then the first missionary impulse rose in my soul." Later, while he was in law school, he made a covenant with a friend. The covenant read, "We resolve to do all in our power for the conversion of the heathen, especially for those for whom nobody else cares."

Now, Zinzendorf has stamped his genius and his commitment to Christ on this Moravian movement. That day he read "Injunctions and Prohibitions" to this small crowd of people, about 300 total, he looked out upon people who were original Brethren, some who were tradesmen, some who were peasants, some who were Catholics, some Lutherans, some Calvinists, and some Separatists. There had been a period of time when there had been severe disputes about predestination, the mode of baptism, and the extent and nature of holiness.

While all this dispute and heated arguments were

going on, Zinzendorf and Pastor Rothe set aside times of prayer. Zinzendorf became burdened for nine young girls in his Bible class who did not know Christ. He felt the nine girls would stay lost as long as those who said they were in Christ kept on fighting with one another. Zinzendorf and Rothe kept holding on to one Bible promise during this period, "I will pour out the spirit of grace and supplication, and they shall look upon Him whom they have pierced" (Zec. 12:10).

When Zinzendorf had finished reading "The Injunctions and Prohibitions" that day, the result was sudden and overwhelming. The people of Herrnhut changed from a group of quarrelling malcontents to a body of orderly Christians. They shook hands and promised to obey the injunctions and prohibitions.

Zinzendorf took a leave of absence from his position in Dresden and moved to the village of Herrnhut.

This all happened in May 1727. That summer was a season of joy, peace, and intense study and prayer. There had been a wonderful outpouring of the Holy Spirit in Silicia. Zinzendorf and Christian David sent word to Silicia and asked for preachers to come to Herrnhut. These men came with messages of fire from God. During the summer, Zinzendorf had discovered at Zittau, in a library, a copy of Comenius's version of the old Church of the Brethren's "Account of Discipline." He made this discovery in July. For the first time in his life Zinzendorf read an authentic account of the old Church of the Brethren, and found they were pure believers of the very truths which he held so dear to his own heart. As he read the words of Comenius, Zinzendorf noticed that the rules set down in the writing of Comenius were almost the same as he had just read to the people of Herrnhut. Zinzendorf returned to Herrnhut, read the treatise to them, and the people were deeply touched. The healing of the wounds of Herrnhut had happened on May 12, 1727. Zinzendorf read the writings of Comenius to them on August 4, 1727.

Pastor Rothe of the parish church in Brethelsdorf invited everyone to come to the Brethelsdorf Church on August 10th for a Communion Service. The people of Herrnhut accepted the invitation. Hardly a seat could be found in the church on that Sunday. Zinzendorf stood and read the "Confession." All at once, everyone in the church was touched with a strange and wonderful power, which no one could explain. They simply felt that the fire of the Holy Spirit had fallen upon them in a definite way. Pastor Rothe felt overwhelmed by a wonderful, irresistible power of the Lord. He sank down to the floor, then the whole congregation fell to the floor. They continued in that service until midnight, praying, singing, and weeping.

I feel sure that we would have been totally satisfied with what happened on that Sunday. We would have shouted, "Glory", and then made out way home. One more thing had to happen to usher in glorious revival.

A little girl had the horrible experience of watching her mother die. Susannah Kuehnel was 11 years old. She was deeply moved by the way her mother had surrendered herself into the Lord's care as she died. Susannah realized that her mother possessed something that she did not have. She entered a time of deep conviction. Susannah struggled deeply for three days. On the night of August 6, 1727, Susannah woke her father at 1:00 in the morning, and said, "Father, I am now a child of God. Now I know how it was and still is with my mother." It was later discovered that three other girls from Zinzendorf's Bible class went through the same experience the same night. Something was happening. (2)

On Sunday, August 10th, the deeply moving service happened in the Brethelsdorf Church. On Tuesday, August 12th, the whole community signed the Brotherly Agreement.

They invited the Lutheran Pastor of the church in Brethelsdorf, Pastor Rothe, to come to the Wednesday service in Herrnhut on August 13th. It was to be a time of celebrating the Lord's Supper, prayer, confession of bad feelings and wrong attitudes. THEN CAME THE MORAVIAN PENTECOST.

"We saw the hand of God and His wonders, and we were all under the cloud of our fathers baptized with their Spirit. The Holy Ghost came upon us and in those days great signs and wonders took place in our midst. From that time scarcely a day passed but what we beheld His almighty workings among us. A great hunger after the Word of God took possession of us so that we had to have three services every day, 5:00 A.M., 7:30 A.M., and 9:00 P.M. Every one desired above everything else that the Holy Spirit might have full control. Self-love and self-will, as well as all disobedience disappeared and an overwhelming flood of grace swept us all out into the great ocean of Divine Love." (3)

Oswald J. Smith said it was the greatest revival since Pentecost. The people could never describe what happened.

The fire of God fell, and they were lost in wonder, love and praise. One man said he did not know if they were on earth or in heaven. David Nitschmann said, "All I know is that from that time on, Herrnhut became a living congregation of Christ." That is revival.

Twenty-seven years later when Zinzendorf preached his famous series of sermons in London, he described that day in August 1727, "We needed to come to the Communion with a sense of the loving nearness of the Savior. This was the great comfort, which was made this day a generation ago. For this day the congregation at Herrnhut was all dissatisfied with themselves. They had quit judging each other because each one had become convinced of his lack of worth in the sight of God and each felt that this communion to be in view of the noble countenance of the Savior, whose sacred head was so wounded. In this view of the Man of sorrows, acquainted with grief, their hearts told them that He would be the Patron and the Priest, who was at once changing their tears into the oil of gladness, their misery into happiness. This firm confidence changed them in a single moment into a happy people which they are to this day. And into their happiness they have since led many thousands of others through the memory and the help which the heavenly grace once given to themselves, so many thousand times confirmed to them since then."

On that day, August 13th, two of the members of the Herrnhut congregation were working twenty miles away. They entered into the same experience at the same time as the people did at the church. The coming of the Holy Spirit at Pentecost and His coming that day at Herrnhut was a community affair. They were all together in one place and were all filled with the Holy Spirit.

James Montgomery, the Scottish Moravian songwriter put that day in verse:

> They walked with God in peace and love,
> But failed with one another,
> While standing for the faith, they strove,
> Brother fell out with brother.

> But He in whom they put their trust,
> Who knew their frames, that they were
> Dust?
> Pitied them, healed their weakness.

> He found them in His House of Prayer,
> With one accord assembled,
> And so revealed His presence there,
> They wept for joy and trembled.

> One cup they drank, one bread they break
> One baptism shared, one language spake,
> Forgetting and forgiven

> Then, forth they went with tongues
> aflame,
> And one blest and delighted,
> The love of Jesus and His name,
> God's children all united.

That love our theme and watchword still,
That law of love may we fulfill,
And love as we are loved.

As great as the blessing of that August day was, there was greater blessing to follow. Four days later, on August 17th, the Holy Spirit was poured out on the children of Herrnhut. The children organized a 24 hour-a-day, 7 days a week prayer meeting. This prayer meeting continued for over 100 years. Can you imagine, in your mind, the small children of Herrnhut bending their knees to the Heavenly Father hour after hour, day after day, year after year. After they started the prayer meeting, adults began to join them, and the prayers of 100 years reaped spiritual blessings untold.

Zinzendorf spoke of this children's prayer meeting, "The children of both sexes felt a most powerful impulse to prayer, and it was impossible to listen to their infant supplications without being deeply moved. The girls and boys held prayer meetings again on the 26th and the 29th of August, and the Spirit of grace and supplication poured out upon the children so powerful that it is impossible to give an adequate description in words."

One of the blessed statements concerning this day of August 13, 1727 was uttered by James Hutton, "As the brethren walked down the slope to the church, all felt that the supreme occasion had arrived. And all who had quarreled in the days gone by made a covenant of loyalty and love. At the door of the church, they entered the building and the service began. The confession was offered by the Count, and then at one and the same moment all dropped in deep devotion and were stirred by the mystic, wondrous touch by a power which none could define or understand. There, they attained at last the firm conviction that they were one in Christ. And, there, above all, they believed and felt that as the twelve disciples at Pentecost had rested the purifying fire of the Holy Spirit."

The timeline of the revival at Herrnhut would be as follows:

May 12, 1727: After a lecture by Zinzendorf, the village signed an agreement to dedicate their lives to the service of Jesus Christ.

July 22, 1727: The community covenanted together to meet often to pray and sing hymns.

August 5, 1727: Count Zinzendorf and twelve or fourteen others spent all night in prayer.

August 10, 1727: Pastor Rothe was so overwhelmed by the Lord that he sank down into the dust. Then the whole congregation followed him. They all continued until midnight in prayer and singing.

August 13, 1727: The Holy Spirit was poured out on the congregation at Herrnhut.

August 17,1727: The children of Herrnhut organized a prayer meeting which went 24 hours a day, 7 days a week. This prayer meeting lasted for over 100 years.

August 26, 1727: Twenty-four men and twenty-four women covenanted together to continue praying in periods of one hour each, day and night.

August 27, 1727: This new prayer meeting started and the intercessors increased to seventy-seven people.

The adult and children's prayer meetings were astonishing. The prayer meetings became known as the Hourly Intercession. The prayer meetings led to action. Thirty-three years after the Herrnhut Pentecost, there were 226 Moravians missionaries scattered around the world. They based these prayer meetings on Leviticus 6:13, "A fire must always be burning upon the altar. It must never go out." This is so difficult to believe. In the tiny village of Herrnhut, Germany began a century of passionate, believing prayer based on the simple belief that God would answer.

This should teach us to come to God in prayer. We must not come pleading with God to send revival, as though He was some kind of reluctant giver, but He is a God who stands ready to answer, and if we come believing, it is a sign that God already has His designs upon us.

How does one explain real revival? I don't suppose any words can ever adequately portray spiritual awakening. Through church history there have been countless revivals. Each revival has had its own characteristics. The revival in England had the fiery preaching of John Wesley and George Whitefield. The New England revival had the staid, solemn preaching of Jonathan Edwards. The Cane Ridge Revival of 1801 in Kentucky had countless preachers on the weekend when the power of God fell. The revival of 1858 began in New York City in a prayer meeting, and continued to be a revival of prayer and great music. The Welsh Revival of 1904 had a young Evan Roberts who did not preach much, but the power of God was on him. The Lewis Revival of 1949-53 had its beginning as two old-maid sisters prayed in their cottage, and one preacher, five farmers and one blacksmith prayed in a little barn.

Every revival throughout church history is unique. No two are exactly the same. God uses different people, different methods, and different times. However, one thing is always the same in times of revival. There is never been great revival without great prayer.

One thing that I always thought was unique concerning the Moravians. They required that every member of the church leave behind a Lebenslaug (literally, life course). This was a short memoir describing his or her spiritual journey. This short story of life would tell of their unredeemed life of sin, their coming into spiritual conviction, their conversion and their new life in Christ. When the person died, a minister would finish the memoir and then read it all at the funeral.

The convictions and beliefs of the dear people of Herrnhut had been hammered out and solidified over the centuries. They include:
The Scripture is the only rule of faith
The Trinity
Original sin
Total depravity of man
The love of God manifested in Jesus Christ
Justification by faith alone, the only necessity of regeneration
Baptism and the Lord's Supper as the only sacraments of the church

The resurrection of the body, judgment, Heaven and hell
We should never forget to thank the Lord for what happened
at Herrnhut in 1727. As we will see in the rest of this writing,
we can trace our spiritual ancestry back to this time. God has
seen fit to open doors of evangelism that has made it possible
for we people in America to hear the gospel, repent of our
sins and come to faith in Jesus Christ because of the faith and
commitment of the Moravians of Herrnhut.

CHAPTER TWENTY

"THE MORAVIANS AND PRAISE"

Praise has always been an integral part of authentic Christianity. Throughout church history, every time great revival broke out, a new spirit, a new song, a new praise came with it. In the 1932 edition of the Methodist Hymnal it says in the opening sentence, "Methodism was born in song." So, too, were the Moravians born in song. When the Holy Spirit fell on Herrnhut in 1727, it opened a floodgate of glorious songs that has never been equaled in Christian history. Praise to the Lord just started flowing out of the Moravians. Praise was an integral part of revival on the Isle of Lewis in 1949-53. The Church of Scotland only sang the Psalms in church services, but when revival came people began to sing and compose great gospel songs on busses, along the beach and working in the fields.

John Wesley started out as a missionary of the Anglican Church. He made his way to America, intending to minister to the Native American Indians. On board the ship, Wesley spent hours learning the German language so he could talk to the Moravians on board the ship. Wesley wrote in his journal on Sunday, October 19, 1735, "Singing with the Germans." His purpose in learning their language was so he might get to know them and learn the secret of the testimony they had in Jesus Christ. Wesley was astounded that these German Moravians could sing praises to God during fierce storms at sea. Wesley wrote, "I began to learn German in order to be able to speak with the Moravians. They are people who have given up all for their Master, and have learned from Him to be modest and lowly, dead to the world, but full of faith and the Holy Spirit."

One of the Moravians on board the ship with Wesley was David Nitschmann. He wrote in his journal, "During the singing session, several subjects were discussed with the English clergyman, among others, the decline and loss of power." Isn't that what we discuss today? Isn't that what we talk about concerning our churches in America today? The loss of power!! Nitschmann continued, " The English parson, John Wesley, misses no opportunity to attend the singing. We wish we could converse easily so we could show him more clearly the way to God."

It was during that famous storm at sea that Wesley became so amazed that not only the Moravian men, but also the women and children were so totally unafraid because of their living experience of faith in Jesus Christ. Wesley wrote in his journal, "Now we can see who has a God, and who hasn't."

Charles Wesley, the brother of John Wesley, wrote 6,000 hymns in fifty years. Peter Bohler, the Moravian evangelist, once told Charles Wesley, "If I had a thousand tongues, I would praise Jesus with every one of them." Shortly after his conversion, Charles Wesley wrote down these words:

Oh for a thousand tongues to sing,
My Great Redeemer's praise,
The Glories of my God and King,
The triumphs of His grace.

He breaks the power of cancelled sin,

He sets the prisoner free,

His blood can make the foulest clean,

His blood availed for me.

The music of the Moravians was deeply rooted in German Pietism. You can see the deep, abiding devotion in the hymns they wrote. "O, Sacred Head So Wounded", My Savior, How Shall I Proclaim", "Angels from the Realms of Glory", "Prayer is the Soul's Sincere Desire."

One of the early-day Moravians was John Cennick. He became a great hymn writer and evangelist. Zinzendorf once called Cennick, "Paul revived." Cennick's parents became missionaries to the West Indies. When John Cennick was converted to Christ, he became a singer of the gospel and a fiery evangelist. Of his conversion, Cennick said he was sitting in a church service, the congregation began singing the 34th Psalm, and he was converted to Christ in an instant.

Revival always inspires praise. It seems that when great revival comes, a fresh filling, a fresh anointing comes from above.

CHAPTER TWENTY-ONE

"MORAVIANS AND THEIR SIN"

When revival comes, it is always a time of exposure of sin. The Word of God will always slice to the deepest part of the soul. When revival comes, no one escapes the probing dagger of the Holy Spirit's holiness.

The two sins that were brought to the surface at Herrnhut were dead formalism in the church and great disunity among the people of the village. The dead state of the Lutheran Church was brought to light. Oh, everything was being done decently and in order, but everything is decent and in order in a cemetery. Even today, in the church, formalism and traditionalism can cover over the fact that we are not right with God, and not right with one another.

The Moravians had no problem at all in believing the right things, but everything was so dead, lifeless, useless. It was only when the Holy Spirit began to move across Herrnhut that the people began to realize that a living union with Jesus Christ was absolutely essential for them, and that living righteous and godly lives with each other was necessary. John Wesley once translated one of the Moravians hymns, "What are our works but sin and death, till Thou Thy quickening Spirit breathes?"

Authentic revival always exposes sin. When we think about sin, we usually think about overt things such as stealing, lying, adultery, murder, etc. How often do we think about the fact that formalism, disharmony, or preaching can be sin in the sight of God? Don't you think that dead religion is as saddening to God as false religion? Don't you think that when Christians talk about one another, or won't fellowship with each other, or gossip about one another, that that grieves the heart of God? Surely when preachers stand in the pulpit and preach with no power from above, that wounds the heart of God as much as fleshly sin.

One time John Wesley was in Germany. He wanted to make a trip to Herrnhut, a journey of 350 miles. A man asked Wesley why he wanted to go to Herrnhut. Wesley replies, "Because that is where the Christians live."

Why do people want to go to your church? Why would anyone want to join your church? Would the answer be, "Because that is where the Christians are?" When Wesley left Herrnhut, he wrote, "I would gladly have spent my life here, but my Master called me to work in another part of the vineyard. I am constrained to make my leave of this happy place. Oh, when will Christianity cover the earth as the waters cover the sea?"

We must always remember that true revival will always bring to the surface the sins in our lives. We should thank God for that.

CHAPTER TWENTY-TWO

"AFTER THE MORAVIAN PENTECOST"

After that eventful day in 1727, Zinzendorf began to organize rules of order for Herrnhut. He issued the rule that all male members of Herrnhut would have a vote in the election of twelve Elders. These twelve Elders would have control over every facet of life in the village. There were rules concerning taxes to keep streets and wells in working order. They established rules for the care of widows and orphans. If any person began to tell tales on other people, the Elders would call them to task. If anyone disobeyed the laws of Herrnhut, the Elders would banish that person. The powers of the Elders were absolute. If anyone desired to live in Herrnhut, the only condition that had to be met was that the person must work and live a godly life. If tramps or beggars came, they could not stay. If a person was lazy, they were ordered to leave. Work was a sacred duty, instituted by God. Zinzendorf said, "We do not work to live, we live to work." Elderly people and sick people could live there in peace.

The workday was sixteen hours a day, five hours of sleep, and the other three hours were spent eating or in meeting. All roving entertainers were forbidden. At Herrnhut, there were no dances, no drinking parties, no games played. If a man got drunk, cursed, fought, or committed adultery or fornication, he was immediately expelled. He was not permitted to return until he shown evidence of true repentance.

No husband could strike his wife and no wife could henpeck her husband.

At this time, Zinzendorf had no idea that the Bohemian Brethren had ever been an independent church. He looked on them as a branch of the Reformed movement. He asked them to look upon themselves as members of the Lutheran Church. They attended the Berthelsdorf Church, took Communion there, had their children baptized there, and their young people were confirmed in the Lutheran Church in Berthelsdorf.

As the months went by, meetings began to increase. All the village was required to attend three meetings each day; at five in the morning they met to sing praises, at dinner time they met, and at nine in the evening they met to sing until bedtime. (1)

Sunday was a full day for the people of Herrnhut. At five in the morning they met for the "morning blessing", from six to nine they met as several choirs, at ten there was a meeting for the children, at eleven was morning worship in the parish church, at one the Head Elder gave a lecture, at three there was a meeting called "strangers' service" for those who had not been able to go to church, at four there was another service at Brethelsdorf, at eight a service in Herrnhut and at nine in the evening, the young men would march around Herrnhut singing hymns. Pastor Schwedler of Gorlitz would sometimes preach a sermon three hours long, and sometimes he would start preaching at six in the morning and preach until three in the afternoon.

For the Moravians, if they read it in the Bible, they

did it. They practiced foot-washing in Herrnhut. Zinzendorf said no one could read the 13th chapter of John without being convinced that this should be done. The practice of foot-washing spread to the Moravians in England and Ireland, but was abandoned in 1818.

As Herrnhut grew, so did the necessity of organization. They began to divide up into "choirs." Martin Linner lived in one house, taught a group of young men. They were known as the "Single Brethren's Choir." This choir was formed in August, 1728. A group of young women, under the leadership of Anna Nitschmann, lived in another house, and formed the "Single Sisters' Choir." The married people began meeting together and formed the "Married Choir." Then, the children were formed into the "Children's Choir."

A few years later, the entire congregation was divided into ten "Choirs"; the married choir, the widowers, the widows, the Single Brethren, the Single Sisters, the youth, the great girls, the little boys, the little girls, and the infants.

A most impressive service was always held on Easter Sunday morning. The entire congregation would meet just before sunrise at "God's Acre", the cemetery. Just as the sun would start to rise, the minister would say, "The Lord is risen." The congregation would exclaim, "He is risen, indeed." Then all the congregation would repeat a confession of faith in Jesus Christ. The Moravians never looked on the cemetery as a place of dread and death. It was always a place of hope in the resurrection, the time when those who lay in the tomb would hear the voice of Jesus Christ, and be caught up to meet the Lord in the air. When a brother or sister died, the

Moravians never spoke of them as dead. They would simply say, "He has gone home."

After that wonderful day of August 13, 1727, the Moravians of Herrnhut developed a strong belief in swift, direct answers to prayer. They made use of the "Lot." By Lot serious church problems were settled, by Lot a woman would determine if she was to marry, by Lot a call to mission service was determined. Once the Lot had been used in any matter, the decision reached by Lot was final and binding.

Another practice that spread throughout the church was the "Cup of Covenant." The "Single Brethren Choir" was reading the Gospel of Luke. As Jesus was sitting with his disciples in the Upper Room, it says, "He took the cup and gave thanks, and said, 'Take this and divide it among yourselves.'" The single brothers pledged obedience to this command, and they passed the cup from hand to hand. When a young man was going out to the mission field, the whole choir would entrust him to the care of the Lord with this simple service. This practice spread to the other choirs. You can hear of this practice in one of the Moravian hymns,

> Assembling here, a humble band,
> Our covenantal pledge to take,
> We pass the cup from hand to hand,
> From heart to heart, for His dear sake. (2)

Life after the Moravian Pentecost was rich, filling and growing for these settlers of Herrnhut. They were getting primed and ready to go out into the world with the gospel of Jesus Christ. Their world began to revolve around three important teachings; Jesus Christ had given his life as a ransom for sin, Jesus Christ had set the perfect example for them to follow, and Jesus Christ was present with them as Head of the Church.

Wherever a Moravian went, he or she was confident that they had been reconciled to God through the death of Christ on the cross, that they were to pattern their lives after Him, and that He would always be with them, no matter what, no matter where.

But, suddenly trouble reared its ugly head. Every time real revival comes, the devil is always quick to make an entrance and do his best to kill the sense of revival. Fast on the heels of the Herrnhut revival many Lutherans began to look on Zinzendorf as a heretic. Zinzendorf was accused of starting a new sect, and being opposed to the teachings of the Lutheran Church. Many looked upon Zinzendorf as a sideshow freak.

Zinzendorf set off down the path of showing that the people of Herrnhut were as true as Martin Luther was himself. Zinzendorf drew up a manifesto in 1729 entitled the "Notariats-Instrument." This document was signed by all the Brethren. Read this document and one can quickly see that Zinzendorf is beginning to think more highly of the Moravian Church. He states that these Moravians of Herrnhut were descendants of the ancient church. They were true heirs of the Church of the Brethren. As the trouble increased, Zinzendorf wanted more and more to fold the Moravian Church into the Lutheran Church.

Smoldering at the core of Zinzendorf's soul was

his missionary zeal. He was invited to attend the coronation of Christian VI, King of Denmark, at Copenhagen. He was warmly welcomed. While there, he saw Eskimos from Greenland and a black man from the island of St. Thomas. It seemed to Zinzendorf that the door to missions had been opened to him. He sent two of the Brethren to Copenhagen, two others to London, one to Sweden, and others to Hungary, Austria, Switzerland, Moravia, the Baltic Provinces, Latvia and Estonia.

One day while Zinzendorf was at Herrnhut, the thought came across his mind that the Brethren would do much better without their ancient constitution. He consulted the Elders. He proposed that they should abolish their regulations, abandon their constitution, cease to be Moravians, and become pure Lutherans. (3)

Zinzendorf never put into print his reasons for wanting to do away with the Moravian Church. This whole issue was submitted to the Lord. Two slips of paper were placed into a box. One slip of paper read, "To them that are without law, as without law, that I might gain them that are without law" (I Cor. 9:21). On the second slip of paper was written, "Therefore, Brethren, stand fast, and hold the traditions which you have been taught" (II Thess. 2:15). Zinzendorf's young son, Christel, drew a slip of paper out of the box, the second slip was chosen by him, and the Moravian Church was saved.

With all the trouble that was brewing, the government finally issued an order that the Schwenkfelders must leave the land, but the Moravians were allowed to stay. The

Schwenkfelders were named after Caspar Scghwenkfeld von Ossig who lived from 1489 to 1561. Through the years these followers of Christ had known severe persecution by governments and state churches. Most of them lived in southern Germany. They were given refuge in 1726 by Zinzendorf. They believed the Bible was the only source of correct theology, but they believed the Bible was dead without the working of the Holy Spirit, just words on a page. They believed that the divinity of Jesus Christ was progressive. Both adult and infant baptism was practiced by them,

When the government issued the decree that the Schwenkfelders must leave, but the Moravians could stay, Zinzendorf became extremely unhappy, for the government had said the Moravians could stay as long as they behaved. He took that as a threat. He took his concern to the Tubingen Theological Faculty and asked them to study and see if the Moravians could keep their discipline and still remain good Lutherans. They came back with the decision that the Moravians were as good Lutherans as there were in the land.

The next year, 1734, Zinzendorf laid out three measures; first, he divided the congregation at Herrnhut into two parts, the Moravian and the purely Lutheran, next, he had himself ordained as a Lutheran clergyman, and third, he sent a few Moravians to found a colony in Georgia (4).

In 1735, Zinzendorf had David Nitschmann set apart as a Bishop. He was a Bishop for the foreign mission field only. Nitschmann set sail for Georgia.

Zinzendorf had no idea that he was so hated by so many people. The Pietists hated him because he had never had a sudden conversion experience that they demanded. He upset his own family by becoming a clergyman. He was of the noble class. He was a Count, and was to mix and mingle with the higher class. The King of Saxony, Augustus III, issued an edict banishing Zinzendorf from his kingdom. He was classified as a heretic. At the same time Zinzendorf was banished from Saxony, a government commission declared that the people of Herrnhut were good Lutherans. The reason for the difference was easy to understand. The government commission said if the Moravians were banished, the government would lose a lot of money in taxes. So, they were declared good Lutherans, but were forbidden to make any new proselytes.

In 1737, the edict of banishment against Zinzendorf was repealed, but the following year it was reinstated, and Zinzendorf was banished from his home in 1738.

CHAPTER TWENTY-THREE

"THE MORAVIANS AND MISSIONS"

By their very nature, revivals are not meant to last. The Day of Pentecost in the Book of Acts did not last. All revival through church history flamed up and then passed away. Revivals are a time of grace, a beginning of great evangelistic activity. When the Holy Spirit came upon that little congregation in Herrnhut in August, 1727, there came a wonderful time of world mission activity. There welled up in the hearts of those Moravians a desire to make Jesus Christ known in all the world. J. Wesley Breddy, the church historian, said when the 18th century opened, and for many years afterwards, there was not a single Protestant missionary in the entire world with the exception of a small group of Moravian Brethren.

Through the years we have called William Carey the father of modern missions. Fifty years before William Carey went to the foreign mission field, the Moravians had missionaries scattered around the world. When William Carey was turned down for foreign mission work, he cried out, "Look what the Moravians have done, and they are poor. Out of loyalty to the Lord we should attempt something."

The Moravians at Herrnhut had their first missionary prayer meeting in January, 1728. This was five months after the Holy Spirit had fallen on them in power. It would seem that the first few months were spent basking in the glow of what God had done for them. Then God began to push them

in definite directions. Within one year of the coming in power of the Holy Spirit, 26 young men had covenanted together
to prepare to go overseas with the message of Jesus Christ.
When Zinzendorf died in 1760, there were 226 Moravian
missionaries scattered around the world.

There is an important lesson here for all of us. God
speaks to a church, and men, women and young people go
out into the world like fire jumping from one place to another. The Spirit of God fell on Herrnhut in 1727. Christian
David, Moravian carpenter, was preaching the gospel in Latvia in 1729, and on to Estonia in 1739. By 1733, there were
Moravian missionaries in Greenland. By 1737, Moravian
missionaries were in Africa. John Smit was in South Africa
in 1737 until he was asked to leave by the Dutch. A short
aside! In 1792 Moravian missionaries were back in South Africa. They came across an old Hottentot man who still possessed a copy of the New Testament that John Smit had given
him. That old man was baptized in 1792. By 1757 there were
Moravian missionaries in Tibet.

It may be that the greatest impact of Moravian missions happened in the West Indies. Anthony Ulrich, a slave
from the West Indies, traveled to Denmark and Germany in
1731. He met some Moravians and told them of the desire of
blacks in the West Indies to hear the Christian gospel. Ulrich
said, "If only some missionaries would come, they would
certainly be heartily welcomed. Many an evening have I sat
on the shore and sighed my soul toward Christian Europe;
and I have a brother and sister in bondage who long to know
the living God." (1) A year later, 1732, two members of the

Moravian Church arrived on the island of St. Thomas and began their work. So eager were they to reach the slaves for Jesus Christ that they figured the only way to get to the hearts of the slaves was for them to become slaves themselves, so they promised they would sell themselves into slavery in order to witness and share the gospel with their fellow slaves. There were 13,000 converts to Jesus Christ in the West Indies before any other missionary had arrived.

The Moravians went everywhere. David Zeisberger spent 60 years of missionary work among the American Indians. Frederich Martin spent his life preaching to the blacks of St. Thomas. Zeisberger and another missionary were thrown into prison for preaching the gospel. Count Zinzendorf and two couples arrived on St. Thomas. As the ship was sailing into port, Zinzendorf said, "What if we find no one here?" One of the co-workers said, "Then we are here." Zinzendorf secured the release of the two missionaries in prison, then wrote back to Germany, "St. Thomas is a much more wonderful miracle than our own Herrnhut. After 14 years Frederich Martin has reached the end of his earthly pilgrimage. More than fifty of his fellow workers have already laid down their lives." (2)

There is an interesting item concerning Moravian missions. They never saw themselves as going out to establish churches or to Christianize a nation. The great idea for them was in winning the first fruits. Their idea was that as many people as possible would go out and win key people to Jesus Christ and then leave them to allow God to work in and through them. They wanted to make Christians, not

Moravians. No one was ever invited to become a Moravian, and anyone who requested to join the Moravian Church was subjected to a severe test, including a probation period of two years. It was much more important for them that you get into Christ rather than get into the church.

CHAPTER TWENTY-FOUR

"THE GOSPEL IN THE CARRIBEAN ISLANDS"

In 1731, Zinzendorf went to Copenhagen to attend the coronation of King Christian VI. While there he met a West Indian black slave named, Anthony Ulrich. Zinzendorf learned of the wretched conditions of the slaves and their deep desire to know about Jesus Christ. He returned to Herrnhut and told the congregation Ulrich's story.

The next year, 1732, came the rise of foreign missions for the Brethren Church. Only ten years before, the bedraggled band of refugees had made their way from Bohemia to Herrnhut. At this time the population of Herrnhut was about 600 souls.

After the meeting in Copenhagen, Anthony Ulrich visited Herrnhut and told the congregation his story, and the longing of his sister and brother to know Jesus Christ. An electric jolt went through one of the men, Leonard Dober. He could not sleep. All he could think about were the poor, black souls of St. Thomas. He went to the Daily Watch-Word that the Moravians read every day. His word for that day was, "It is not a vain thing for you because it is your life, and through this thing you shall prolong your days." (1)

The young men of Herrnhut usually took walks late in the evening. One evening as Dober was walking along with Tobias Leupole, he shared his feelings about a call to go to St. Thomas. Leupole replied that he was feeling the same call. They wrote a letter to Zinzendorf, sharing their feelings about this call. Zinzendorf read the letter to the congregation, but did not share the names of the two men. The idea met with immediate opposition. Some thought the idea was reckless, while others thought it was an attempt to gain fame. Finally, the Brethren decided to submit the proposition to the Lot.

What an important meeting! For the first time in the history of Protestant Europe, a congregation of believers had decided to undertake the job of preaching the gospel of Jesus Christ to the heathen. The Lot was taken and decided that Dober should go, but that his friend Leupold should stay. Dober then chose as his traveling mate, David Nitschmann.

This is the same David Nitschmann who walked into Herrnhut in 1724 with four friends. They had come from Bohemia, on their way to Poland. They observed what was happening in Herrnhut and decided to stay. These five men were a part of the old Bohemian Church. David Nitschmann became a Bishop of the new church in Herrnhut. (2)

On August 21, 1732, at 3:00 in the morning, these two men waited in front of Zinzendorf's house, waiting for him to take them to Bautzen. Zinzendorf had spent the entire night in prayer.

Dober and Nitschmann left Herrnhut with three dollars each in their pockets, and a bundle on their backs. They were going to Copenhagen, a distance of 600 miles.

When they arrived in Copenhagen, they began to meet opposition and ridicule from many different people. Finally the royal chaplains gave them enough money to pay their fare and to obtain the tools of their trade. The Queen gave them aid, and Princess Amelia gave them money and a Dutch Bible. (3)

The gift of this Bible proved to be of God, for the slaves of St. Thomas spoke Dutch and the two men on the voyage took the opportunity to learn that language.

Their ship set sail on October 8, 1732, five years after the coming of the power of the Holy Spirit on Herrnhut. When Dober and Nitschmann landed at St. Thomas, they went in search of Anthony Ulrich's sister. They found her, with her husband and brother on a plantation. They read a letter to her from her brother, Anthony. In this letter was the quotation, "This is life eternal, that they might know thee, the only true God, and Jesus Christ whom thou has sent." (4)

The two men began preaching the gospel to the slaves. Nitschmann was a carpenter and was able to secure work to support himself. Dober was a potter, but was unable to find clay suitable for the work of a potter. It was not long until Anthony's sister and her husband became believers in Jesus Christ.

A few months later, Nitschmann had to return to Europe. Dober stayed on St. Thomas. He labored alone for 16 months, not hearing anything from Herrnhut. One evening, Dober was sitting by the fire, when , suddenly three men stood before him. One was Tobias Leupold, the same man who had volunteered to go with Nitschmann three years before. In 1735, Dober returned to Herrnhut, having been appointed an Elder by the church. Dober was chosen as the Chief Elder of the Moravians. It was a position in which

the Chief Elder was to know all about every person in the
Moravian community. Dober found this impossible to do.
He resigned as Chief Elder, stating that he found the job impossible. The Moravians, in studying this matter, came to the
conclusion that no man could perform the job as Chief Elder.
They decided that only Jesus Christ should be Chief Elder of
the Church. It was decided that the matter would be decided
by the Lot. In a basket were placed two slips of paper, one was
written, "Yes", and the other slip contained the word, "NO."
When the Lot was taken, the slip of paper with the word,
"Yes", was chosen. Since that time, Jesus Christ has served as
the Chief Elder of the Church. Also, since that time, even to
the present, when there is an important meeting of the heads
of the Church, there is always an empty chair at the meeting,
signifying that the Chief Elder, Jesus Christ, sits in that chair,
and is attending the meeting.

Opposition and persecution soon came into play. All
preaching and conversation with the slaves became totally
forbidden. There soon followed several false charges against
the Moravian missionaries, and they were thrown into prison in 1738. From their prison cells the Moravians would pray
and sing praises to God. The slaves would gather outside their
cell windows and join in with their singing. In 1739, Zinzendorf arrived on St. Thomas. He found all the missionaries in
prison. The next day they were set free.

Zinzendorf stayed a few short weeks on St. Thomas.
During that time he preached to the slaves for two weeks,
and 800 of them were converted to Jesus Christ.
Some of the plantation owners became very upset. They

did not want the slaves to become Christians because they thought the slaves might become better Christians than they were.

According to the reports, nine hundred slaves at this time were under conviction, and interested in being saved. Many slaves would come every night to be taught, and on Saturday night a large gathering of slaves would meet and be taught until 7:00 Sunday morning. There are different reports of baptisms. On one occasion, forty slaves were baptized, on another, ninety were baptized

One of the missionaries, Frederick Martin, wrote in 1740, "Hardly a day passes on which we are not visited by persons bemoaning their sins and crying for mercy. When taking a walk, we hear them pray and weep, one in a sugar-field, another behind a bush, and a third behind his hut, imploring the Lord to cleanse them from their sins and pollutions." (5)

The Moravian missionaries moved from St. Thomas to St Croix, forty-five miles south of St. Thomas, The work there was severe and difficult. In the first fifteen years of missionary work on these two islands, fifty Moravian missionaries were buried in their soil.

One of the interesting converts on the island of St. Croix was a black man named, Cornelius. He could speak Creole, Dutch, German and English. He managed to purchase freedom for himself and his wife, and finally for his six children. For forty-seven years he was an assistant in the Moravian mission. White men would sit and listen to him preach. When Cornelius was eighty years old, he called his children and grandchildren around his bed and said, "If you follow this advice of your father, my joy will be complete when I shall see you all again in bliss, and be able to say to our Savior, 'Here, Lord, is your unworthy Cornelius and the children whom you have given me.' I am sure our Savior will not forsake you: but, I beseech you, do not forsake Him." (6)

The gospel of Christ, preached by the Moravians went from St. Thomas to St. Croix, to St. John to Jamaica, to Antigua, to Barbados, and to St. Kitts. There were over 13,000 converts to Christ before a missionary from any other church came to the islands.

CHAPTER TWENTY-FIVE

"THE GOSPEL IN SOUTH AMERICA"

It is almost impossible for those of us who live today to realize the attitude of the Church toward the savage races in the world in the 1700s. Rev. A.C. Geekie, the minister of St. Stephen's Presbyterian Church in New South Wales wrote concerning the savage races, "Europe, especially Britain, would fain save him, but he cannot be saved. Born a savage, meant for savage life, it would seem as if his Creator had decreed that his continuance should be limited to this state; and that the approach of civilization, and the races who pertain to it, speak the doom of savagism and the savage." (1)

However, the Moravians of Herrnhut paid no attention to this method of thinking. They simply believed the gospel of Jesus Christ was meant for the whole world. After the Moravians had spread the gospel to the Caribbean Islands, they turned their face 200 miles toward the south to the nation of Guiana. At that time, Guiana was divided into three sections; the English, Dutch and French Guiana. The main focus of the Moravians was on Dutch Guiana which is known today as the Republic of Suriname. This small Dutch colony is on the northeastern tip of South America. It is bordered on the east by French Guiana, Guyana to the west and Brazil to the south. On the country's north coast is the capital city of Paramaribo.

In 1734, Spangenberg, Bishop of the Moravian Church, made a trip to England. He passed through Holland and had meetings with the Dutch Trading Company for Suriname. The Moravians decided to form colonies of missionaries in this small country. The next year, 1735, three Moravian missionaries made their way to Dutch Suriname. The Moravians founded a little colony west of Rio de Berbice, one hundred miles from the coast. They called their colony Pilgerhut, and began working with the Arawak Indians. For the first eight years, the task seemed hopeless. By the time ten years had passed, forty-five persons had been converted and received into the church.

The colonial government sent out an order that all converts had to be clothed, and a tax had to be paid on each one of them. Two of the converts were drafted into military service. Many of the Indians of Pilgerhut retreated into the forests.

By 1756, Pilgerhut had grown to a colony of 233 people, which did not include children. At this point there had been 300 conversions to Jesus Christ. One of those converts, who wished to write to the Moravians in Europe, dictated a letter, "Having arrived at manhood, I spent many years without any knowledge of my Savior. When I afterwards became desirous to experience what I had heard, it was granted me. Jesus has cleansed me in his blood, and delivered me from my disobedience. This truth, that he died and shed his blood for me, has conquered and captivated my heart. This I can never forget; and therefore will I love him with all my soul, and daily give my heart to him." (2)

Soon the Herrnhut Moravians sent out missionaries to the town of Paramaribo. In 1747 a Moravian station was established at the west end of Dutch Guiana, and was given the name of Ephraim. Another station was set up called Sharon. A number of the blacks who lived in the forest attacked Sharon, killed some and set fire to everything. Sharon was eventually abandoned.

In Dutch Guiana, runaway blacks became numerous. They lived in the forests as fugitives. They became known as Bush Blacks. By the time the Moravians had arrived, thousands of them lived in the forests of Dutch Guiana. Work among this group was almost impossible. Finally, by a miracle of God, Arabi, the chief of the Saramacca Bush Blacks, became the first convert to Jesus Christ. In his village, the alligator was worshipped as a village god. Arabi went to the river, and delivered this message to the alligator, "I intend to shoot you. Now, if you are a god, my bullet will do you no harm; if you are a mere creature, it will kill you." (3)

Slowly, slowly, through the years, the work of the Moravians bore fruit. By 1815, the number of black believers in Christ amounted to 663 souls.

In 1828 a large new church building was erected in Paramaribo. A new church building was built in Charlottenburg for which the church members donated 1200 florins, which would be $240,000.00 in today's money. (4)

By 1881, the Moravian mission in Dutch Guiana had proven the most successful. There were, in that year, 73 missionaries and 21,683 converts to Jesus Christ.

CHAPTER TWENTY-SIX

"THE GOSPEL IN GREENLAND"

In 1731, Zinzendorf visited Copenhagen to attend the coronation of King Christian VI. The King was a personal friend of Zinzendorf. While in Copenhagen, Zinzendorf met two Eskimo boys from Greenland who had been baptized by Hans Egede, the Danish missionary. Zinzendorf learned that the Dutch mission to Greenland had been abandoned. When he returned to Herrnhut, he told the church what he had discovered about Greenland. One of the Moravian men, Matthew Stach, was deeply touched by what he had heard. In the cemetery at Herrnhut, he shared the feelings of his heart with Frederick Bonisch. They wrote a letter to the Herrnhut Church telling of their desire to go to Greenland. Quite a long period of time went by before there came any answer from the church. When the answer came, Frederick Bonisch had gone on a journey, and Christian David said he would take the place of Bonisch in Greenland. This is the same Christian David who had made his way from Moravia with a small group of people to first populate Herrnhut, the same Christian David who was the first to put an ax to a tree to begin building the first house of Herrnhut. Matthew Stach said, "We had nothing but the clothing on our backs. We had been used to make shift with a little, and did not trouble our heads how we should get to Greenland or live there." (1) Both of these men, Stach and David, came from solid, strong Christian families. Both of their fathers had suffered greatly in Moravia because of their faith.

On January 11, 1733, Christian David, Matthew Stach and one of Matthew's cousins set off on their journey to Greenland. In Copenhagen they met with resistance. People could not understand how they would live, where they would live, or what they would eat. Count von Plesss became quite impressed with these three young men. He gave them wood with which to build a house and fifty dollars for them to use.

In April, 1731, the three young men embarked on a voyage of six weeks to Greenland. "All we can reasonably infer is that there exists one vast, dreary glacier expanse, devoid of beast, bird, or insect, a Sahara of ice instead of sand, where not even a moss or lichen appears. An awful silence reigns, broken only when the stormy wind arises.....John David, an English explorer in the sixteenth century, christened it "The Land of Desolation." (2)

These three young men had come to this land of desolation to preach the gospel of Jesus Christ to the Eskimo. Little did they know that it would be five long years before they would see the first convert to Jesus Christ. The Moravian missionaries had come to a land of frigid cold to bring the warmth of Jesus Christ to their souls. The Eskimos called themselves, "Inuit" which is plural for "innu." "Innuit" means "people." One tribe that lived on the upper coast of Greenland thought they were the only people living on the face of the earth.

Christian David and the two Stachs found a people who lived in filth. Their clothes were covered with grease to ward off vermin. They ate enormous amounts of food, as much as ten pounds of meat per day. A man would lie on his back and his wife would feed him until he could eat no more. They ate mostly seals, raw and fat. The seal not only provided them with food, but clothing, covering for their boats, oil for their lamps.

The Eskimos believed in spirits, both good and evil. The chief spirit, Torngarsuck, lived in a mansion underground. Above the earth is the upper world, and, after death, souls go up or down. The Eskimos preferred to go down when they died because it would be warm. They had an absolute horror of annihilation.

One of the difficult jobs the Moravians had in Greenland was trying to get across to the Eskimos the idea of forgiveness. There was no word in their language for forgiveness. Their solution to this problem was to make a word. They compounded a word, using several Eskimo words to let them know the meaning of forgiveness. The word they came up with was, "Issumagijoujungnainerik." That word in the Eskimo language means, "Not-being-able-to-think-about-it-anymore." Is it not wonderful to know that if you have been saved through Jesus Christ, as far as your sins are concerned, you don't have to think about them anymore? They are forgiven.

To this region of the world came the Moravians. They had to gain access to these people who did not want them there. They had to learn the language. They had not been in Greenland long until a devastating sickness came. This could have been a reason for the Moravians to give up and go home, but they were determined to stay for years, "if only to save one soul."

During their second year, two more Moravians came to Greenland, Frederick Bonisch and John Beck.

The Moravians decided they would teach the Eskimos dogmatic theology. They began with the fall of man in the Book of Genesis. The result was abject failure. One evening, John Beck was talking to a group of Eskimos. He stopped his teaching on dogmatic theology, and began to read a Scripture, "And being in an agony, He prayed more earnestly, and His sweat was as it were great drops of blood falling down to the ground." One of the Eskimos, Kajarnak, ran to the table and said, "How was that? Tell me that again, for I, too, would be saved." (3)

From that time on, the Moravians forgot about dogmatic theology and told the story of the arrest, trial, scourging, and Jesus Christ on the cross for the sins of man. They found that the power was in the story of the cross of Christ. The Eskimos became eager to hear and learn.

At one time the missionaries did not hear a word from Herrnhut for two years. At times they were at the point of starvation. They ate raw seaweed.

Kajarnak became a devoted follower of Jesus Christ. He began to tell the story of Jesus to his people and they became more and more interested. In 1741, when Kajarnak was on his deathbed, his people were gathered around him, and he told them, "Don't be grieved about me; have you not often heard that believers, when they die, go to our Savior, and partake of his eternal joy? You know that I am the first of you that was converted by our Savior; and now it is his will that I should be the first to go to him." (4)

The year, 1738, was a pivotal year in the world of missions and the message of Jesus Christ. It was in this year that missionaries on St. Thomas were thrown into prison. It was in this year that George Whitefield made his first trip to America to preach. It was in this year that David Brainerd came to faith in Jesus Christ. It was in this year that John and Charles Wesley found peace with God through Jesus Christ. It was in this year that the light of the gospel began to shine on Greenland.

In 1881, there were nineteen Moravian missionaries on Greenland, and the churches numbered 1,545 converted Eskimos. The society of the Eskimos changed. They became a civilized, docile people. Kindness and order reigned in their villages. Formerly, old, sick Eskimos were left out on the cold steppes to die, but after Christ came to Greenland, the Eskimos began caring for their elderly.

William Cowper wrote a song concerning the Moravian mission,

> Fired with a zeal peculiar, they defy
> The rage and rigor of a polar sky,
> And plant successfully sweet Sharon's rose
> On icy plains and in eternal snows.

CHAPTER TWENTY-SEVEN

"THE GOSPEL IN AMERICA"

During the 1730s, so many Moravians were going out across the world as missionaries that the ideas of the course the missionaries were to follow became very vague. They had no idea what their duties might be. They would go to a place to which they felt God had called them, with no idea where they would live, how they would eat, nothing in their minds and hearts but trust in God.

The 1730s surely was a whirlwind for the Moravians of Herrnhut. Suddenly they were going everywhere, in every direction. The missions of the 1730s included St Thomas (1730), Greenland (1732), Suriname (1735), Georgia (1735), South Africa (1736), Gold Coast (1736), Switzerland (1740), England (1740), South Africa (1742), Wales (1743), Maryland (1745) Jamaica (1754), India (1760), and other mission trips too numerous to list.

Because there was no written rules or duties of the missionaries, each one worked alone, trying to do the will of God as he or she saw fit. In 1738 the Moravians wrote and published "Instructions for All Missionaries."

Zinzendorf spoke concerning these instructions, "You are to not to allow yourselves to be blinded by the notion that the heathen must be taught first to believe in God, and then afterwards in Jesus Christ. It is false. They know already that there is a God. You must preach to them about the Son. You must be like Paul, who knew nothing but Jesus and Him crucified. You must speak constantly, in season, and out of season, of Jesus, the Lamb, the Savior, and you must tell them that the way to salvation is belief in this Jesus, the Eternal Son of God." (1)

The Moravian missionaries went forth, not teaching theology, not bent on doctrine, not different theories concerning the atonement, but they taught and preached the sacrifice of Jesus Christ on the cross. Bishop Spangenberg said, "We must hold to the fact that the blood and death of Jesus are the diamond in the golden ring of the gospel."

In 1735, John Toltschig and Anthony Seiffart, accompanied by Bishop Spangenberg made their way from Herrnhut to America. They came to Georgia. Another company of Moravians, headed by David Nitschmann, joined them. It was aboard the ship coming to Georgia that a horrible storm buffeted the ship. On this ship were two Anglican missionaries, John and Charles Wesley. During the storm, shipwreck seemed definite. John Wesley wrote in his journal, "At seven I went to the Germans (Moravians). I had long before observed the great seriousness of their behavior. Of their humility they had given a continual proof by performing those servile offices for the other passengers, which none of the English would undertake; for which they desired and would receive no pay, saying, 'It was good for their proud hearts', and 'their loving Savior had done more for them.' And every day had given them occasion of showing a meekness, which no injury could move. If they were pushed, struck or thrown down, they rose again and went away; but no complaint was found in their mouth. Here was now an opportunity of trying whether they were delivered from the spirit of fear, as well as from that of pride, anger and revenge. In the midst of the Psalm wherewith their service began, the sea broke over, split the main-sail in pieces, covered the ship and poured in between the decks, as if the great deep had already swallowed us up. A terrible screaming began among the English. The Germans calmly sung on. I asked one of them afterwards, 'Were you not afraid?' He answered, 'I thank God, no.' I asked, 'But were not your women and children afraid?' He replied mildly, 'No, our women and children are not afraid to die.'" (2)

When the ship finally reached Georgia, John Wesley sought out Bishop Spangenberg to talk to him about spiritual matters. Wesley wrote of this conversation in his journal. Spangenberg spoke to John Wesley, " 'My brother, I must first ask you one or two questions. Have you the witness within yourself? Does the Spirit of God bear witness with your spirit, that you are a child of God?' I was surprised, and knew not what to answer. He observed it and asked, ' Do you know Jesus Christ?' I paused and said, 'I know that He is the Savior of the world.' He replied, 'True, but do you know He has saved you?' I answered, 'I hope He has died to save me.' He then said, 'Do you know yourself?' I said, 'I do.' But I fear they were vain words." (3)

John Wesley stayed in Georgia for two years. On the way back to England, Wesley wrote, "I went to America to convert the Indians, but, oh, who shall convert me? Who, what is he that will deliver me from this evil heart of unbelief? I have a fair-summer religion. I can talk well; but let death look me in the face, and my spirit is troubled. Nor can I say, 'To die is gain.'" (4)

When Wesley returned to London, it was his encounter with Peter Bohler, a Moravian, that changed his life forever. John Wesley was born again and turned England upside down for Jesus Christ.

The Moravians had not been in Georgia for a long time when war broke out between Spain and England. The English authorities of Georgia asked the Moravians to register for military service. Since the Moravians were pacifists, they refused. The result of this was the Moravians left Georgia and migrated to Pennsylvania in 1738 and 1739.

Bishop Spangenberg went to Pennsylvania for a while, but then returned to Herrnhut and told of the open door to the Native American Indians. The one who led the way in this endeavor was Christian Henry Rauch. He arrived in New York in 1740, and met a trio of Mohegan Indians; Tschoop, Choop and Shabash. All three were drunk. He followed them home, which was about fifty miles south of Albany, New York. The Indians knew some of the Dutch language, so Rauch was able to share the gospel of Christ with them, and two of these men were converted to Christ.

The Indian man, Tschoop, wrote a letter, "I have been a poor wild heathen, and for forty years as ignorant as a dog. I was the greatest drunkard and the most willing slave of the devil; and, as I knew nothing of our Savior, I served vain idols, which I now wish to see destroyed by fire. Of this I have repented with many tears....Now, I feel and believe that our Savior alone can help me by the power of his blood, and no other. I believe that he is my God and my Savior, who died on the cross for me, a sinner. I wish to be baptized, and long for it most ardently." (5)

Tschoop once gave a talk. He said, "I know how heathen think. Once a preacher same and began to explain that there is a God. We answered, 'Do you think us so ignorant as not to know that? Go back from where you came.' Another preacher came and began to teach us. He said, "You must not steal nor lie nor get drunk.' We answered, 'You fool, do you think we do not know that? Learn yourself first, and then teach the people to whom you belong to leave off these things. For who steals or lies, or is more drunken than your own people?' After some time, Brother Christian Henry Rauch came into my hut, and sat down by me. He spoke to me, "I come to you in the name of the Lord of heaven and earth. He sends to let you know that he will make you happy, and deliver you from the misery in which you lie at present. To this end, he became a man, gave his life a ransom for man, and shed his blood for him.' When Rauch had finished, he lay down upon a board , and fell into a sound sleep. I thought, 'What kind of man is this? There he lies and sleeps. I might kill him, and then throw him out into the wood, and who would regard it? But this gives him no concern. I could not forget his words. Even when I was asleep, I dreamed of that blood which Christ shed for us. I found this to be something different from what I had ever heard. Through the grace of God, an awakening took place among us....I say, therefore, Brethren, preach Christ our Savior and his sufferings and death, if you would have your words to gain entrance among the heathen."

Rauch kept preaching. A Christian congregation was established in 1742. There were thirty-one baptized Indians.

The New York Assembly passed two laws, one requiring all persons to take the oath of allegiance, or leave the province. The other law, requiring Moravians to cease from further teaching or preaching. The sheriff closed the mission church.

The Moravians packed up and moved to Pennsylvania. The Christian Indians followed them, except for seventy-one of the Indian believers.

Now, there are the Moravians who had come from Georgia and the Moravians who had come from New York, all together in Pennsylvania. They founded a settlement and named it Bethlehem. Today, Bethlehem, Pennsylvania is the most important Moravian site in America.

Probably the greatest missionary to the Native American Indians among the Moravians was David Zeisberger. He was born in Moravia, came with his parents to Herrnhut, followed them to Georgia, and now is a student at the little college in Bethlehem, under the teaching of Bishop Spangenberg. Zeisberger lived and preached among the Indians for sixty-three years. He lived like an Indian, dressed like one, received an Indian name and became a member of an Indian family. Zeisberger became known as the "Apostle to the Indians."

Zeisberger founded many Indian Christian settlements among the Six-Nation Indian Tribe, the Delaware Tribe, and the Iroquois. He mastered the Delaware and Iroquois languages. He had printed books in their languages which included the Lord's Prayer, the Ten Commandments, different Scripture passages, and a Harmony of the Gospels.

While Zeisberger was at his height as a missionary to the Indians, the War of Independence between America and England broke out. Both sides urged the Indians to fight on their side. Zeisberger urged the Indians to be neutral. One day, the American Colonel Williamson appeared in the Indian village of Gnadenhutten. He disarmed all the Indians, accused them of having sided with the British and decided to put the whole congregation to death. The village was set on fire, the Indians were given a few minutes to pray, then the soldiers began the work of butchering the Indians. When the horrible work was finished, there were ninety bodies lying in blood. This became known as the Blood-Bath of Gnadenhutten. (7)

This blood-bath destroyed the Indian Mission. It left the work of Zeisberger in ruins. In 1808, as Zeisberger lay on his death-bed, the Indian converts gathered around his bed and sang him home to glory with hymns he had translated from the Ancient Brethren's hymn book.

CHAPTER TWENTY-EIGHT

"THE GOSPEL EVERYWHERE"

To write of all the mission work the Moravians did would take a book hundreds of pages long. All I will be able to do in this work is touch on the multitude of missions that the Moravians achieved in the fruitful years of Moravian Missions.

When the Holy Spirit fell on the little congregation at Herrnhut in 1727, it seemed a fire was instantly ignited in their hearts to tell the world about Jesus Christ. Education, finances and convenience made no difference. They were compelled to go into all the world and tell the story of Jesus Christ, and His death on the cross for the sins of the whole world.

These plain, unadorned disciples, who had escaped severe persecution in Moravia, took, quite literally, the closing words of Jesus, "All authority has been given to Me in heaven and on earth. Go therefore and make disciples of all the nations, baptizing them in the name of the Father and of the Son and of the Holy Spirit, teaching them to observe all things that I have commanded you, and lo, I am with you always, even to the end of the age." (Matthew 28:18-20)

Those Moravians who went out to the mission field were supported in every way by those who stayed at home. Every man, woman and child who stayed behind in Herrnhut knew they were an integral part of spreading the gospel around the world. Every missionary who

went out carried with them no more than a knapsack on
their back and a message in their hearts about Jesus Christ.

They went to:

Sweden	1727
German Territories	1728
Denmark	1731
St. Thomas	1730
Greenland	1732
Suriname	1735
Georgia	1735
South Africa	1736
Gold Coast	1736
Netherlands	1737
Norway	1737
Pennsylvania	1737
Switzerland	1740
Ceylon	1740
England	1740
New York	1740
Algiers	1741
Connecticut	1742
New Jersey	1743
Wales	1743
Maryland	1745
Ireland	1746
Persia	1747
Egypt	1752
North Carolina	1753
Jamaica	1754
India	1760
East Indies	1777
Mongolia	1854
Tibet	1854
Jerusalem	1867

And, this is not all. There were many scouting trips, inquiries and short-term mission trips to other places in the world. By the end of the 1700s, the Herrnhut congregation had 300 missionaries around the world.

On that blessed day, August 13, 1727, when great power fell on the tiny congregation, that day when "they hardly knew if they had been on earth or in heaven", one person recorded the following:

"Loud weeping and cries to heaven nearly drowned out the singing. The service did not end until, as Zinzendorf described it later, true "Herzensgemeinschaft" (communion of the heart) had descended upon them all. Where they had been one body before, now they were one in spirit, the Spirit of Christ....Those who had seriously annoyed each other, now embraced and promised to serve one another in peace, so the whole congregation came back to Herrnhut as new-born children." (1)

If you ever visit Bethlehem, Pennsylvania, you can go to the old cemetery, which is called, "God's Acre." You can stand there and remember the day when Moravians around the world would gather on Resurrection Morning (Easter Sunday). They would gather and sing with the sure hope that someday those who were buried there will be raised from the dead, along with them. They would stand there and praise the Lamb who was slain for them. It is easy to think of the famous motto of Count Zinzendorf, "May the Lamb that was slain receive the reward of His suffering."

CHAPTER TWENTY-NINE

"SOLDIERS IN A COMMON CAUSE"

I wanted to devote one chapter in this book to those who were instrumental in spreading the gospel of Christ around the world. I call them soldiers in a common cause. Odd? Yes! The Moravians were pacifists. They refused to enter military service. However, I call them soldiers because they were soldiers of the Cross. They entered the battle for the souls of men, women and young people. So, I invite you to take a look at some of the soldiers in a common cause.

—⁓—

CHRISTIAN DAVID

Christian David was born in 1690 In Moravia. He was a Roman Catholic who was deeply superstitious. He spent quite a lengthy time with deep trouble in his soul, wrestling with questions for which he had no answers. Until he was twenty years of age, he never had seen a Bible. His patron saint was St. Anthony. He thought he was doing everything right. He always knelt down before every statue and picture of the Virgin Mary.

He grew up as a shepherd boy. For all his zeal and all his piety, he was not sure that he himself had escaped the snare of the fowler. (1)

He found a small group of Protestants who told him that the Pope was the Antichrist, that the worship of saints was useless, and that only through faith in Jesus Christ could a person be saved. First, he was shocked, then puzzled. He watched as some of his Protestant friends were arrested and thrown into a prison call. He crept up close to the window of their cell and heard them singing praises to God.

Christian David began reading. He would read Lutheran books and Catholic books. He read and read until, finally, he decided he could not believe either one of them. He finally came to the place where he hated the name of Christ. For a while, he consulted some Jews. They tried to convince him that the New Testament was nothing.

David then turned to the Bible. In 1710, when he was twenty years old, he came to deep conviction that Jesus Christ was the Messiah. He went to Hungary, and finally came to Berlin where he became a member of a Lutheran Church.

Whatever he was looking for, he did not find in the Roman Church, nor the Protestant group in his hometown, nor in the Lutheran Church of Berlin. He left Berlin and joined the Prussian Army. When he was discharged from the army, he made his way to Gorlitz, and came into contact with two Pietist clergymen, Schafer and Schwedler.

Christian David found peace with God through the Lord Jesus Christ. He married a member of Schwedler's church. For the next five years, he made his home in Gorlitz. He made several trips back to Moravia to tell his old Protestant friends of the new life he had found in Jesus Christ. He became known as the Bush Preacher, and, because of his preaching, Moravia became a hot-bed of revival.

When Christian David returned to his home area in Moravia, he became acquainted with several German families; the Schneiders, Nitschmanns, Stachs, Zeisbergers, Jaeschkes, Neissers, and the Grassmanns. These families knew the Lord, and had suffered greatly because of their faith. The Neissers' old grandfather, George Jaschke, had been a godly patriarch of this family for years. When George Jaschke was on his death-bed, he called his sons and grandsons to his bedside, and told them, "It is true that our liberties are gone, and that our descendants are giving way to a worldly spirit, so that the Papacy is devouring them. It may seem as though the final end of the Brethren's Church had come. But, my beloved children, you will see a great deliverance. The remnant will be saved. How, I cannot say; but something tells me that an exodus will take place; and that a refuge will be offered in a country and on a spot where you will be able, without fear, to serve the Lord according to His holy Word." (2)

Through a series of circumstances and meetings, Christian David had met Count Zinzendorf. He asked the Count for permission to bring persecuted Protestants from Moravia to Berthelsdorf. Zinzendorf told Christian David if they came he would find a place of refuge for them.

At ten o'clock at night, on May 27, 1722 Christian David met with a little small group in the home of Jacob Neisser. They opened the door of the house, marched out of Moravia toward Berthelsdorf, Germany. They arrived at the estate of Count Zinzendorf on June 8, 1722.

It was Christian David who cut down the first tree at

Herrnhut in order to build a house.

Today, there is only one monument in Herrnhut. On this monument is this inscription, "On this spot was felled the first tree for the settlement of Herrnhut, June 17, 1722. Psalm 84:3, 'Yea, the sparrow hath found an house, and the swallow a nest for herself where she may lay her young, even thine altars, O Lord of hosts, my King and my God." (3)

Christian David made ten more trips back to Moravia to bring other people to Herrnhut. It was Christian David who, along with another man, made his way to the frozen landscape of Greenland to serve as a missionary among the Eskimos. It was Christian David who stood as a bulwark in the Moravian Church for years and years.

Christian David died in 1751. If you walk into "God's Acre" today, that little cemetery in Herrnhut, as you walk through the gate, the first gravestone you see is that of Christian David. There would never have been a Herrnhut without this man, Christian David.

—ᴡ—

AUGUST GOTTLIEB SPANGENBERG

Benjamin Franklin once said, "My very much respected friend, Bishop Spangenberg." (4) We would do well to look into the life of this amazing man to ascertain what he accomplished during his life.

Spangenberg was born in 1704 in Klettenberg. His father was the local Pastor. He became an orphan at the age of thirteen, went on to the University of Jena to study law, but very soon switched from law to theology. He got his degree in 1726 and began teaching theology in Jena.

In 1728, Zinzendorf visited Jena and met Spangenberg. In 1730, Spangenberg visited Herrnhut, was very impressed, and established a program of caring for the sick and poor in Jena. The Jena authorities closed this program down because it had not been sanctioned by the state.

Spangenberg accepted a position as superintendent of schools, which was connected to his orphanage at Halle. He assumed this position in 1732. However, differences arose and the Senate of the Theological Faculty gave Spangenberg a choice; he could do penance, submit to his superiors, separate from Zinzendorf, or he could leave the matter to the king. The case went to the king, who ordered the military to expel Spangenberg from Halle. He left Halle in April, 1733, went to Herrnhut and cast his lot with the Moravians for the next sixty years.

The first thirty years of his work was devoted to missions in Germany, England, Denmark, the Netherlands, Suriname, and Georgia.

The next thirty years of his work with the Moravians was spent, largely, in Pennsylvania. When Zinzendorf died, Spangenberg was called back to Herrnhut to work on the organization and administration of the Moravian Church.

In 1777, Spangenberg wrote the "Compendium of the Christian Faith of the United Brethren." This became the standard when considering Moravian doctrine. For instance, there was much division on the matter of Calvinism, especially the belief of double predestination, that is, people are predestined to salvation and people are predestined to damnation. Spangenberg wrote, "If we sum up that which has been deduced from the Scripture concerning the Father, Son and Holy Ghost, we may answer the question, Whether God would have all men to be saved, with a confident, Yes. There is in him the most fervent desire, and the most earnest will that we all should be saved. Would God command all men everywhere to repent, and yet would not, that all men should be saved? Who can form such a thought of the God of Holiness and Truth?" (5)

When Spangenberg was called back to Herrnhut at the death of Zinzendorf, he spent the rest of his life there, dying at Berthelsdorf in September, 1792. He was buried in Herrnhut at "God's Acre."

It was this man who founded the first Moravian Church in England, the one in Fetter Lane. It was this man who led the first mission effort in Yorkshire. It was this man who was on the front lines of the work in America. It was this man who wrote so much defending the Moravians. It was this man who led the Moravians through so many difficult financial crises. On one occasion, Kant, the philosopher, was told by a student that his philosophy did not bring peace to the heart. Kant replies, "Peace! Peace of heart you will never find in my lecture room. If you want peace, you must go to that little Moravian Church over the way. That is the place to find peace." (6)

Throughout most of the sixty years of ministry of August Spangenberg, the Moravians called him, "Brother Joseph," signifying that they looked upon him as Joseph of the Old Testament, who looked after and cared for his brothers.

—᙭—

LEONARD DOBER

Dober was born in 1706 in Swabia, Germany. He learned the trade of potter from his father. At the age of seventeen he went to Herrnhut and was converted to Christ. When Zinzendorf returned from Copenhagen and told the people of Herrnhut about the black man he had met and the condition of the slaves on St. Thomas, Dober felt a call to go to St. Thomas as a missionary. Tobias Leupold wanted to join Dober in this mission effort. At first, the Moravian Church opposed their going. They decided to leave the results up to the Lot. Leupold's Lot said that he must wait. Dober's Lot read, "Let the lad go, for the Lord is with him." Dober and David Nitschmann were chosen to go to the Caribbean as missionaries.

Dober and Nitschmann left in 1732, and had certain success on St. Thomas. Dober returned to Herrnhut in 1734 and began serving as Chief Elder of the Moravian Brethren. In 1741 he realized he could not keep up with all the work, and offered to resign. This brought about the decision of the Moravian Church to declare that Jesus Christ is the only Chief Elder of the Church.

Dober married Anna Schindler in 1738, but she died during childbirth in 1739. In 1743 he married again to Anna Engel. He was consecrated a bishop of the church and served in Livonia, England, Holland, and Silesia. When Zinzendorf died in 1760, Dober returned to Herrnhut where he served on the board of directors of the Moravian Brethren. He spent his last years in Herrnhut and died in 1766, and is buried in "God's Acre."

—ᴍ—

DAVID NITSCHMANN SR.

There were two David Nitschmanns instrumental in the work of the Moravians. This David is the older of the two men.

Nitschmann was born in Moravia in 1676. His father held meetings in his house every week, where the house was filled with people singing songs from the ancient Brethren's song book, and then a sermon would be read. When David was sixteen years old, both of his parents died within two days. In 1700 David was married to Anna Schneider, a marriage that lasted for thirty-five years and was blessed with four children. One son, Melchior, ended up in prison for his faith and was martyred in Moravia. His daughter, Rosina made the move to Herrnhut with her husband. The other two children were Johanna Nitschmann and Anna.

In 1704 David moved to Kunewald. He met several ancient Brethren. He visited them, held meetings with them, taught them.

In 1724 Christian David came to Kunewald. David heard Christian David preach a sermon, went home and told his wife and children what Christian David had said. A great awakening began in Kunewald and the surrounding villages. One Sunday, more than 150 people came together in David's house. His son, Melchior, preached a sermon. A local official came and took all of their books. About twenty of the fathers of the homes were arrested and thrown into prison. A few days later they were released.

Seven weeks later, David Nitschmann gave to the offi-
cials the testimony of his faith. He was declared a heretic and
thrown into prison. His last hours in prison are described to
us in his own words:

"January 24, on a Thursday night, I said to my Brethren, 'I will take my leave of you tonight.' David Schneider
immediately said, 'If you go, I cannot stay here. I want to go
with you.' I said to him, 'I won't tell you that you must come,
but if you are sure, you can come with me.' It stayed at that;
we waited until the eleventh hour of night, I was worried how
my chains would be loosed. I gripped my knife in my right
hand, and with my left I took the lock, which was strong and
new, and as I held it, the lock was already open. My eyes filled
with tears of joy. I said to David Schneider, 'thus I see that it
is the Savior's will that we should go.' We took the irons from
our feet in the room where we were, silently said farewell to
the other Brethren, and searched over the yard to find a ladder. I went to the gate, which was closed every night with two
doors, and there stood the first door open. I went out into the
hall, and there the other door stood open as well, which was
the other sign that we should go forward. As we came out of
the castle, we laid our irons by the wall and went through the
garden, and then into my house, where I told my wife how
she should behave when I should send someone to pick her
up, and then went in the night the five miles to Oderberg,
where we stayed three days. Thus I turned my back on my
enemies, and the Savior rescued me from their land." (7)

David and his family came to Herrnhut in 1727, about
the time of the great awakening of 1727. He was in Herrnhut for

eight years until he received a call to serve as a missionary on St. Thomas and St. Croix. He returned to Herrnhut in 1737. Finally, he received a call to go to Pennsylvania with his daughter Anna. He spent the last years of his life yearning for the growth of the Brethren and the conversion of the Indians of America.

David Nitschmann passed away in 1758 at the age of eighty-two. On his deathbed, he told a friend, over and over again, "Now my little hour will soon come." He passed away quiet, composed and surrounded by friends. He is buried in "God's Acre" in Bethlehem, Pennsylvania.

―⁓―

ANNA NITSCHMANN

Anna was born in 1715 in Moravia. She served as the Chief Eldress of the Moravian Church for most of her life. She began serving at the age of 14. She served as a spiritual mentor and counselor to the female members of the church. When Count Zinzendorf's first wife passed away, he married Anna in 1757. Both of them died within twelve days of each other. Anna is buried in "God's Acre" at Herrnhut.

―⁓―

DAVID ZEISBERGER

David Zeisberger was born in 1721 in Moravia, and moved with his family to Herrnhut in 1727. When his family went to Savannah, Georgia to the new Moravian settlement, David stayed behind to finish his education. In 1738, he came to Georgia and rejoined his family. From there he moved to the Moravian settlement in Pennsylvania. He labored for sixty years among the Native American people.

Zeisberger was the founder of Schoenbrunn, the first white settlement in Ohio. He established the first school and church in the state of Ohio, wrote a history of the American Indians and published several books in the Delaware Indian language.

In November, 1808, Zeisberger's health began to rapidly decline. On the day he died, the local Indians gathered in his room, and sang songs to him. About 3:30 in the afternoon, he sighed and breathed his last breath.

Zeisberger was buried in the cemetery at Goshen, Benjamin Mortimer preached the funeral sermon in English, using Revelation 12:11 as his text, "And they overcame him by the blood of the Lamb, and by the word of their testimony; and they loved not their lives unto the death." While Rev. Mortimer preached in English, John Henry, an Indian convert, translated the sermon into the Delaware language.

On David Zeisberger's grave is a marble slab with this epitaph, "This faithful servant of the Lord labored among the American Indians as Missionary, during the last 60 years of his life."

—⚏—

JOHN CENNICK

John Cennick was born in 1718. He grew up in the Anglican Church. As far as we know, Cennick had never heard of the Moravians nor the Methodists while growing up. When Cennick was nine years old, he heard his dying aunt say, "Last night the Lord stood by me and invited me to drink of the fountain of life freely and I shall stand before the Lord as bold as a lion." These words stayed with him through the years. When he was seventeen years of age, he came to the time when he had been under deep conviction of sin for two long years. He had prayed nine times a day, fasted, given money to the poor, but he found himself almost going mad in his fear of death and the judgment day. Finally, in his pew at the St. Lawrence Church, he heard the voice of Jesus say, "I am thy salvation." In that moment, John Cennick felt himself converted to Christ. (8)

Through a series of circumstances, Cennick came in contact with John Wesley. He joined the Methodist movement. He became a teacher upon the recommendation of John Wesley. At an open-air meeting, the preacher did not show up, and Cennick was asked to preach. He became one of Wesley's lay preachers.

Eventually Cennick and Wesley had a falling out over the doctrines of Calvinism and the doctrine of sinless perfection. "Cennick was not quite in affinity with Wesley. Wesley's fierce and uncompromising Armeninism, Wesley's constant and bitter tirades against Calvinism, turned Cennick' thoughts to Whitefield. But, perhaps, Cennick's main objection to John Wesley's type of religion arose from the doctrine of sinless perfection and Calvinism . (9)

After Cennick separated from John Wesley, he joined the ministry of George Whitefield from 1740-45. Wherever

Cennick went to preach, he addressed great crowds and was attacked by furious mobs. At Upton-Cheyny the villagers armed themselves with a horn, a drum, and a few brass pans, made the echoes ring with their horrible din, and knocked the preachers on the head with the pans, a genius put a cat in a cage and brought some dogs to bark at it, others hit Cennick on the head and hurled dead dogs at him. (10)

Cennick went to Exeter in southwest England to preach. The opposition was so fierce and horrible that Cennick wrote a booklet about his experiences there. The booklet is entitled, "An Account of a Late Riot at Exeter."

Following I want to share with you a small
example of what happened at Exeter:

"After this I prayed our Savior to take care of us, and then we went out, the Brethren going before. I believe now more than a thousand men, women and children were at the door, ready to use us ill. The Three-Tun Tavern, which was over against us, was crowded with gentlemen, and all the windows of the houses, on both sides of the street; and the streets adjoining were filled with spectators. I believe such rioting and noise were never before on a Sunday in Exeter. Our brethren were hardly out, but they began pushing them down, and the sisters the same, tearing their clothes, spitting upon them, and daubing them with dirt, and thus they served old and young, women and children, some of whom were terrified and hurt, but the most part behaved with the greatest meekness in the world, so that some of the sort were moved with compassion, and a gentleman coming by had pity on us, and stayed and shared with us, till all were helped out....At this time a good many were hurt, among whom was Penelope Hill, who was thrown down several times, and kicked very much. Also Mrs. Paramore was struck again on her breasts and bruised badly, and narrowly escaped being tumbled about in the dirt. Robert Williams was beaten and kicked on his belly severely by Mr. P----ke, Mr. L—th—y, and others." (11)

This booklet that Cennick wrote is twenty-nine pages long, and contains many terrible things the believers had to endure while Cennick was preaching and after.

§

In 1746, Cennick became a Moravian preacher. Some Baptists who were visiting London heard Cennick preach and invited him to come to Ireland to preach. In Ireland he founded 220 Moravian societies between 1747 and 1752.

While in Ireland, many of the local clergy complained to their Bishop that Cennick was emptying their pulpits. The Bishop told them, "Preach what Cennick preaches, preach Christ crucified, and then the people will not have to go to Cennick to hear the gospel." (12)

At the time of his preaching power, he broke down in body and in mind. He suffered from mental depression. He left Ireland and arrived in London at Fetter Lane with a high fever and totally exhausted. There he died on July 4, 1755, at the young age of thirty-six.

—∞—

JAMES MONTGOMERY

James Montgomery was born in Ayrshire, Scotland in 1771, the son of a Pastor and missionary of the Moravian Church. While he was in school at Fulneck, his parents left England and became missionaries in St. Thomas in the West Indies.

After sampling several jobs as he grew up, Montgomery finally became the assistant of Joseph Gales, publisher of the Sheffield Register. In 1794 Montgomery took over the Register, changed its name to the Sheffield Iris and continued to edit it for 31 years.

Montgomery is best known as a poet and writer of hymns. He wrote over 400 hymns. Some of his most famous hymns are: "Spirit of the Living God", Angels from the Realms of Glory", "Songs of Praise the Angels Sing", and "Come Ye That Fear the Lord."

—∞—

PETER BOHLER

Peter Bohler was born in 1712 and became a Moravian missionary and a bishop of the Moravian Church. He went to the University of Jena in 1731 and studied under Count Zinzendorf. Eventually Bohler became a Moravian and served as a missionary in Georgia and Pennsylvania. He was instrumental in the founding of the towns of Nazareth and Bethlehem in Pennsylvania.

It was this man, Peter Bohler, who was so deeply connected to the conversion of John and Charles Wesley. They
both had returned from a stint as Anglican missionaries
in Savannah, Georgia. Both were depressed, disillusioned,
doubting if they really knew the Lord. In London they ran
into Peter Bohler in January, 1738. Long and earnest discus-
sions and arguments finally resulted in John Wesley's conversion to Christ in May, 1738 at Aldersgate. Let us allow John
Wesley to tell of this in his own words:

"In my return to England, January, 1738, being in im-
minent danger of death, and very uneasy on that account,
I was strongly convinced that the cause of that uneasiness
was unbelief, and that the gaining a true, living faith was
the one thing needful for me. But still I fixed not this faith
on its right object: I meant only faith in God, not faith in
or through Christ. Again, I knew not that I was wholly void
of this faith; but only thought I had not enough of it. So,
when Peter Bohler, whom God prepared for me as soon as
I came to London, affirmed of true faith in Christ, (which is
but one), that it had those two fruits inseparably attending
it, dominion over sin, and constant peace from a sense of
forgiveness, I was quite amazed, and looked upon it as a new
gospel. If this was so, it was clear I had not faith. But I was
not willing to be convinced of this. Therefore I disputed with
all my might, and labored to prove that faith might be where
these were not; especially where the sense of forgiveness was
not: for all the scriptures relating to this , I had been long
since taught to construe away, and to call all Presbyterians
who spoke otherwise. Besides, I well saw no one could (in

the nature of things) have such a sense of forgiveness, and not feel it. But I felt it not. If then there was no faith without this, all my pretensions to faith dropped at once.

When I met Peter Bohler again, he consented to put the dispute upon the issue, which I desired, Scripture and experience. I first consulted the Scripture, but when I set aside the glosses of men, and simply considered the words of God, comparing them together, endeavoring to illustrate the obscure by the plainer passages, I found they all made against me, and was forced to retreat to my last hold, 'that experience would never agree with the literal interpretation of those Scriptures. Nor could I allow it to be true till I found some living witnesses of it.' He replied, 'He could show me such at any time; if I desired it, the next day.' And accordingly the next day he came with three others, all of whom testified of their own personal experience that a true living faith in Christ is inseparable from a sense of pardon for all past, and freedom from all present sins. They added with one mouth, that this faith was the gift, the free gift of God, and that he would surely bestow it upon every soul who earnestly and perseveringly sought it. I was not thoroughly convinced, and by the grace of God I resolved to seek it unto the end: 1. By absolutely renouncing all dependence, in whole or in part, upon my own works or righteousness, on which I had really grounded my hope of salvation, though I knew it not, from my youth up. 2. By adding to the constant use of all the other means of grace continual prayer for this very thing- justifying, saving faith; a full reliance on the blood of Christ shed for me; a trust in him as my Christ, as my sole justification, sanctification, and redemption." (13)

John Wesley had come a long way from his time as an Anglican missionary in America. He had struggled long and hard over his sins. Wesley wrote in his diary, "I found my brother at Oxford recovering from his pleurisy; and with him Peter Bohler; by whom (in the hand of the great God) I was, on Sunday, the 5th, clearly convicted of my unbelief; of the want of that faith whereby alone we are saved. Immediately it struck into my mind, 'Leave off preaching. How can you preach to others who have not faith yourself?' I asked: 'But what can I preach?' Bohler said, 'Preach faith till you have faith.' Accordingly, Monday, 6th, I began preaching this new doctrine, though my soul started back from the work. The first person to whom I offered salvation by faith alone, was a prisoner under the sentence of death." (14)

Charles Wesley had more than 6,000 hymns published after he was converted to Christ in 1738. On one occasion, Peter Bohler told Charles Wesley, "If I had a thousand tongues, I would praise Jesus with every one of them." (15) Shortly, Charles Wesley wrote his immortal lines:

> Oh, for a thousand tongues to sing
> My Great Redeemer's praise
> The glories of my God and King
> The triumphs of His grace
>
> He breaks the power of canceled sin,
> He sets the prisoner free
> His blood can make the foulest clean
> His blood availed for me.

Peter Bohler was made superintendent of the Moravian Church in England, then was ordained as a Bishop in the Church. Bohler spent the last nine years of his life in England. He died in London in 1775 at the age of sixty-two.

—⚹—

COUNT LUDWIG VON ZINZENDORF

Zinzendorf was born in 1700 n Dresden. He became a religious reformer and Bishop of the Moravian Church.

The Zinzendorf family was a noble family of Lower Austria. As a result of the Reformation, the family became Lutherans. When Zinzendorf was six weeks old, his father died, and he was sent to live with his grandmother, Henriette Catharina von Gersdorff. This grandmother did much to shape the character and future of Zinzendorf.

He spent his school days at Halle, and in 1716 he went to the University of Wittenberg. He bought the estate of Berthelsdorf from his grandmother, appointed Johann Rothe as Pastor of the church and John Heitz as manager of his estate.

In 1722, Zinzendorf offered a corner of his estate as an asylum for persecuted Christians from Moravia and Bohemia. The settlement was called Herrnhut. After a period of conflict and disagreement, Zinzendorf visited the people, calling upon them to love one another. In May, 1727 he read to the people of Herrnhut a paper he had written, "The Brotherly Agreement." This paper described how Christian life should be in a community. On August 13, 1727, a powerful, life-changing revival took place in the village of Herrnhut. In 1732 the Moravian Church in Herrnhut began sending out missionaries, first to the island of St. Thomas, then South America, then Greenland, then out into the rest of the world.

Zinzendorf visited America in 1741. He came to Pennsylvania where he met Benjamin Franklin and leaders of the Iroquois Tribe.

In 1756 Zinzendorf's wife, Erdmuthe Dorothea, died, and in 1757 he married Anna Nitschmann. Anna had been the spiritual leader of the Moravian women for many years. Three years later, 1760, Zinzendorf became ill and died. His wife, Anna, died 12 days later.

Of all of the papers I have read concerning Count Zinzendorf, the one that made the deepest impression on me was a lecture he gave in Berlin in April, 1738. This has come to be known as "Zinzendorf's 'I Believe'":

I believe that my Savior, my King, bears His name with
    honor and glory.
I believe His eternal divinity.
I believe His real humanity.
I believe that I am one of His household.
I believe that I was lost. I have known the sentence of
    death. But, I believe most certainly that I have
    been ransomed and absolved.
I believe that I am the just reward of all His labor, of
    all His pains and sweat.
I believe that He has won and gained me by His own
    sword and bow.
I believe that I am no longer compelled to sin.

I believe that I will not die.

I believe that I have mastery over the Devil.

I believe that I am redeemed, not through word or
       work, or miracle or arbitrary decree of God,
       or through a new creation or through any other
       means than through the punishment of death
       which the Son of God suffered for me.

I believe that I now belong to no one but to Him who
       has earned me.

I believe that He has the Kingdom over all.

I believe that I live under Him, where I am under His
       protection, under His peace, under His rule.

I am certain that I have the unalterable right, which all
       my fellow citizens have, to be as unchangeably
       holy as they, and that I am as constantly happy
       as they all are.

I also believe that I am nothing without Him, and that
       I live only because He lives. As long as He lives,
       I will live also.

And, I know all this as certainly as I know that my
       head is on my shoulders. (16)

CHAPTER THIRTY

"THE SECRET TO REVIVAL"

It is so difficult to speak or write about authentic, genuine revival. What brings revival? Who starts revival? Both are good questions, but the answers are hard. Some believe revival is an act of a Sovereign God who just picks out a place and sends revival to that location. Others believe revival is in the words of II Chronicles 7:14, "If My people, who are called by My name shall humble themselves, and pray, and seek My face, and turn from their wicked ways, then will I hear from Heaven and will forgive their sins and heal their land." There are people who believe that if you just do A,B,C, and D, then, wham-o, revival comes. Perhaps it is somewhere in the middle of these two thoughts. I believe in the Sovereignty of God. However, I am like the old Scottish Highlander preacher, Duncan Campbell. Campbell said, "I believe in the Sovereignty of God, but I don't believe in any doctrine of sovereignty that nullifies the responsibility of man." (1)

A man once commented, "In all my journeys I have found only three objects that exceeded my expectations; the ocean, Count Zinzendorf and the Herrnhut congregation." (2)

There are several things that contributed to the great revival at Herrnhut. They are all important. One does not negate the others. It is as if each item is like a finely sewn quilt. The pattern in the quilt is not complete without each piece in the quilt.

—w—

THE EXALTATION OF JESUS CHRIST

I am sure the Moravians would have placed this right in the center of their quilt. Revival always exalts Christ. It is impossible to understand the Herrnhut revival without having some understanding of their strong, strong emphasis on the person of Jesus Christ. When Jesus told his disciples that the Comforter was coming, He said, "He shall glorify Me." The theology of the Moravians became Christology. Their creed was Jesus Christ. The entire road the Moravians traveled was characterized by a warm, deep devotion to Jesus Christ. Zinzendorf said, "I have one passion. It is Jesus. Jesus only."

If we, in our modern world, will ever come back to the place where we truly exalt Jesus Christ in our lives, our homes, our churches, perhaps revival might come again to our thirsty land.

Is this where revival begins? Is revival coming when we, once again, center on the Person of Jesus Christ? Does not the Scripture say, "If any man love not the Lord Jesus Christ, let him be anathema."? Is real revival just falling in love with Jesus Christ all over again?

Down through church history, the church fathers were always worshipping the Father, the Son and the Holy Spirit. It is almost as if the Moravians bypassed all of that. They wrote hymns, prayed, preached, and prayed all about Jesus Christ. They exalted Jesus Christ in every facet of their lives.

Did not our Lord even say about the Holy Spirit, "He will glorify Me."?

The words of the poet still ring in our hearts:
Where is the blessedness I knew when first I saw the Lord?
Where is the soul-refreshing view of Jesus in these words?
What peaceful hours I once enjoyed,
How sweet the memory still,
But they have left an aching void the world can never fill.

The reason the world can never fill the aching void in our hearts is because our souls are bigger than the world. God has placed eternity in our souls, and the only thing that can fill our souls is to be constantly in love with Jesus Christ.

—⚏—

THE CENTRALITY OF THE CROSS

When the Moravians thought about Jesus Christ, they always saw Him as a lamb led to slaughter for their transgressions and bruised for their iniquities. To the Moravians, it was always the cross, the cross, where Jesus shed his blood for the sins of the world.

It was the suffering of Jesus, the wounds of Jesus, the blood of Christ that held the Moravians in awe. Their theme, over and over again, was the Cross of Christ, the wounded Lamb of God. The Catholics look to the crucifix. The Moravians always had the mental image of the crucified One. Jesus Christ was constantly before the throne, pleading for sinners in his glorified body.

When Zinzendorf was ordaining missionaries, at some point he would always ask the question, "Brother, dost thou know His wounds?" He was talking about identification with Jesus Christ in His death on the Cross. Martin Luther once said, "If you would know God, you must find Him in the wounds of Christ."

When Zinzendorf was preaching in London, he preached a series of 16 messages. Some of the quotes from those messages:

"Christians are God's people begotten by His Spirit, obedient to Him and kindled by His fire, His blood is their glory. In every degree and phase of our spiritual life and growth and service the blood of Jesus is indispensable." (3)

"The blood of Christ is not only the sovereign remedy for sin, it is also the chief nourishment of the Christian life." (4)

"Our preaching of the wounds may not produce many sudden conversions, but they will be thorough and they will be lasting." (5)

The centrality of the Cross of Christ goes all the way back when Zinzendorf spent the day in the art gallery in Dusseldorf. He was so transfixed as he stood before the painting of the crucified Christ. He said after that day all he could talk about was the blood of Christ, the cross of Christ, the wounds of Christ, the Lamb of God slain before the foundation of the world.

During the Welsh Revival of 1904, the preacher during that great movement of God was a 26 year-old man named Evan Roberts. Roberts had a favorite saying that he repeated over and over again, wherever he went, "Remember the blood! Catch the flame." The centrality of the cross of Jesus Christ will always be important in any revival.

—⚭—

THE LOVE OF THE BRETHREN

Speaking of love of the brothers, Jesus once said, "By this shall all men know that you are My disciples." It is impossible for revival to come on any people if there is rancor, disagreement, turmoil, bitterness, strife, or any such thing in the hearts of the people.

It has always been very interesting to me that the people of Herrnhut had reached a place of discord, bickering, harsh disagreement, but, in May, 1727 they came to that night when they laid all of that down, and became friends, brothers and sisters in Christ, and began to love one another. Three months later, the Holy Spirit fell in great power on that little congregation. It should not be surprising that He came to them when they began loving one another.

When Zinzendorf lay dying, his last words to his family were, "I am gong to my Savior. I am ready. There is nothing to hinder me now. I cannot say how much I love you all. Who would have believed that the prayer of Christ, 'that they all may be one', could have been so strikingly fulfilled among us? I only asked for first-fruits among the heathen, and thousands have been given me. Are we not as in Heaven? Do we not live together like the angels? The Lord and His servants understand each other. I am ready." (6)

If we ever climb out of our chasm of luke-warmness in our churches today, one of the first things we will have to do is come back to a total love for the brethren. Revival can-

not come without that. Revival will not come without that.
May the Dear Lord place in our hearts a genuine love for all
the saints.

—⚒—

TOTAL SURRENDER

One cannot read the story of the Moravians without being deeply impressed by their total surrender to Jesus
Christ. Their whole life centered around Him. One man said,
"In all my journeys I have found only three objects that exceeded my expectation; the ocean, Count Zinzendorf, and
the Herrnhut congregation." (7)

When I first began this section of the manuscript, I
intended to title this section, "Total Commitment." I changed
my mind when I discovered the difference between the
words, "commitment" and "surrender."

The definition of commitment is, "An act of committing to a charge or trust, an agreement or pledge to do
something in the future." The definition of the word, "surrender" is, "to yield to the power, control or possession of
another upon compulsion or demand, to give oneself up into
the power of another."

It is very clear from a study of those early Moravians that they were not committing themselves to do something either now or in the future. Commitment carries with
it the idea of doing something, working for something. The
Moravians were only interested in the fact that they had surrendered themselves. They had given themselves up into the

power of another, Jesus Christ. Their lives were not lives of working, trying to gain the favor of God. Their lives were lives of surrender, totally giving up themselves into the control and power of another.

The lives and ministry of the Moravians reminded me so much of the old hymn, "I Surrender All."

All to Jesus I surrender
All to Him I freely give;
I will ever love and trust Him
In His presence daily live.

All to Jesus I surrender
Make me, Savior, wholly Thine,
Let me feel the Holy Spirit
Truly know that Thou art mine.

More than 4,000 people attended the funeral of Count Zinzendorf at Herrnhut. On his tombstone are inscribed these words, "Here lie the remains of that immortal man of God, Nicholas Lewis, Count and Lord of Zinzendorf and Pattendorf; who through the grace of God and his own unwearied service, became the ordinary of the Brethren's Church, renewed in this eighteenth century. He was born in Dresden on May 26, 1700, and entered into the joy of His Lord at Herrnhut on May 9, 1760. He was appointed to bring forth fruit, and that his fruit should abide." (8)

Every man, woman and child of the Moravian congregation rose in the morning to greet Jesus Christ, lived through each day with Him as their thought, and went to bed at night thinking of Him who had died on the cross for their sins. Surrender and commitment were not just two words to these dear people. It was a living, breathing way of life for them.

Today, one of the largest gatherings of Moravians is in Fetter Lane in London. Dr. F. B. Meyer, the great Pastor of London once wrote, "Those of you who visit London might very well walk down from Holborn to Fleet Street by a little street which is known as Fetter Lane. When you are half-way down Fetter Lane, on your left hand you will see a very simple doorway, and over it the words, 'Moravian Chapel.' Whenever I go down that street I stop there for a moment and lift my hat." (9)

Why is Fetter Lane so important? Well, for one thing, John Wesley learned all he knew from those godly people. That is the place where John Wesley met with Peter Bohler, a Moravian. When Wesley returned to Aldersgate Street he met 40 or 50 people at 5:00 in the afternoon in the Fetter Lane Chapel. John Wesley was there, also Charles Wesley and George Whitefield and a number of others. They waited on God and, suddenly, they became quite conscious of the presence of the Holy Spirit. They fell on their faces, overcome with gratitude to God. They then rose and began to sing. John Wesley said that he felt his heart strangely warmed.

The total surrender to Jesus Christ that the Moravians had kept spilling out on other people. When you trace the movement of the Spirit of God from Herrnhut, to London, to America, you can safely say that we have had the opportunity to come to Christ because of the surrender and commitment of the Moravians.

Would it not be proper for us to use that small question that Count Zinzendorf asked of each missionary as he or she was being ordained? "Do you know His wounds?"

Are you seeking to be a full-time Christian worker? Do you know His wounds?

Are you a deacon, an elder? Do you know His wounds?

Are you a Sunday School teacher, trying to teach the Bible week after week? Do you know His wounds?

Are you a choir member, singing up front Sunday after Sunday? Do you know His wounds?

Are you a church member, attending church, and going through the motions week after week? Do you know His wounds?

Are you a young person, going to concerts, clapping your hands, trying to be joyful? Do you know His wounds?

Are you a child and feel left out? The Moravian children started a prayer meeting that lasted for 100 years. Do you know His wounds?

Count Zinzendorf had a life motto, "I have one passion, it is Jesus, Jesus only." (10)

Count Zinzendorf wrote several hymns during his life. One of those hymns he wrote:

> Rise, go forth to meet the Lamb,
> Slumber not midst worldly care;
> Let your lamps be all on flame,
> For His coming now prepare.
> Then when'er you hear the cry,

Lo, the Bridegroom draweth nigh,
You will not confounded be,
But can meet Him joyfully.

Let us walk the narrow way,
Watchful, cheerful, free from toil,
Trim our lamps from day to day,
Adding still recruits of oil,
Doubly doth the Spirit rest
On His happy peaceful breast,
Who himself to praying gives,
Who a life of watching lives. (11)

—∞—

PRAYER

If one takes time to study the revivals of church history, one common denominator will be found; prayer. Every great revival has had as its common core a few people who set themselves to prayer. They prayed, then kept on praying until God did something in a marvelous way.

For instance, in the Lewis Revival of 1949-53, there were nine people who gave themselves to prayer, and God came down in a glorious way. There were two old-maid sisters; Peggy Smith and Christine Smith who prayed in their humble cottage night after night. There was the Pastor of the Barvas Church, James Murray Mackay and six of the men of his church; Kenneth Macdonald, Roderick Macleod, Sandy Macdonald, Angus Macleay, Colin Macleod and John Smith.

These seven people prayed in a little barn north of the Barvas Church until the fire of God fell and changed the Isle of
Lewis.

I can still remember growing up as a boy on a farm in
western Oklahoma. We would listen on the radio to a preacher from Oklahoma City, Dr. E. F. Weber. Every day when he
would come on the air, he would open with the same statement, "God is still on His throne, and prayer changes things."

Revival will never come unless a few people are willing to pay the price in prayer. The Moravians knew that, believed that, and went to God in prayer and stayed there.

Prayer in the life of the Moravian community was a
natural, wonderful, necessary discipline. One can trace the
importance of prayer very early in the life of Count Zinzendorf. When he was in the college at Halle at the age of 16,
he took to Professor Franke a list of seven praying societies
he had formed. Zinzendorf carried with him, throughout his
life, an atmosphere of prayer.

When the tiny village of Herrnhut was settled in
1722, there were very few people who lived there. In the next
five years many others began to arrive, until, in 1727 the population of Herrnhut was about 300 souls. By the time 1727
arrived, the people of Herrnhut were sharply divided with
dissension and bickering. Revival was nowhere in sight for
the Moravians.

Then began what the Moravians called, "the golden
summer of 1727." Zinzendorf was fully aware of all the bickering, hatred, and division in the village. On May 12, 1727,
Zinzendorf called a meeting of all the citizens of Herrnhut.

He spoke to them about unity, love and at the end he said that everyone who wanted to stay in the village would have to sign an agreement which contained 42 articles. This contract was about living their lives together and the spiritual life of the village. In this contract they were to choose 12 elders by lot, have daily gatherings, sing praises to God , enter into prayer, and have small group Bible studies.

This agreement was signed by all the people on May 12th. For the following three months, a spirit of prayer enveloped the groups that Zinzendorf had formed. The prayer meetings began to grow. On August 5th the first "nightwatch" was held. On August 12, 1727, Zinzendorf called the entire village together for an all-night prayer meeting,

Suddenly, the village of Herrnhut exploded on August 13, 1727 when the Holy Spirit came to them in great power. This day, August 13, 1727, has been called, "The Moravian Pentecost." The Herrnhut Church had come together for a Communion Service and the fire of God fell on all of them, young and old.

Fourteen days later, August 27th, twenty-four men and twenty-four women made a covenant with each other to spend one hour each day in prayer. The next week the children of Herrnhut organized and began a children's prayer meeting. This scheduled, organized prayer meeting lasted for over 100 years.

They first decided on a place to pray. If you visit Herrnhut today there is a shaded street that leads to the cemetery. "Over the entrance, on the outside, is this inscription, 'Jesus is risen from the dead', and on the inside, 'He is become the first fruits of them that sleep." The nearest grave on the left is that of Christian David, whose name has an honored place in Moravian history….The hill bears the name of Hutberg……From this commanding point one enjoys a wide view over the Moravian domain." (12)

It was on top of this hill called Hutberg, which means, "watch-mountain", that the Moravians began their 100-year prayer meeting. They organized this prayer meeting so that three people were praying on Hutberg every hour of every day. Stop and think about that for a minute! There are 168 hours in a week. The Moravians had 168 one-hour slots to fill with three people at all times. Let us stretch our minds for a bit. The Moravians in Herrnhut, and then their missionaries around the world went to the Lord in prayer constantly; 168 hours per week, 672 hours per month, 8064 hours per year. In 100 years they prayed to the Lord 806,400 hours, almost one million hours spent in prayer asking God to send revival to them and to the parts of the world where their people were sharing the message of Jesus Christ. No wonder revival came to them.

This small group of 300 Moravians in the first 15 years after the Holy Spirit fell on them at Herrnhut sent out 70 missionaries to the uttermost parts of the world, to the unreached people. They learned their languages, lived as they lived, suffered greatly and told them about Jesus Christ.

On the mission field, wherever the Moravians labored, prayer was an integral part of their daily life. "It is an interesting circumstance that, even in the earliest Moravian labors at Shekomeko (1743), daily meetings were held and a monthly prayer-day established, when account of mission progress in different parts of the world were communicated, and petitions offered in behalf of all men." (13)

"The Memorial Days of the Renewed Church of the Brethren", published in 1822, ninety-five years after the decision to initiate the prayer watch, quaintly describes the move in one sentence: 'The thought struck some brethren and sisters that it might be well to set apart certain hours for the purpose of prayer, at which seasons all might be reminded of its excellency and be induced by the promises annexed to fervent, persevering prayer to pour out their hearts before the Lord.'" (14)

The springboard of this continual prayer meeting came from the heart of Count Zinzendorf. In one of the community prayer meetings, Zinzendorf felt that the Lord was highlighting Leviticus 6:13, "Fire shall be kept burning continually on the altar; it is not to go out." Zinzendorf had a strong feeling that the prayers of the saints should continually rise up to God, like a holy incense.

There were two main focal points in this Moravian prayer time. First, to lie prostrate before His throne both day and night, offering to Him the sacrifice of praise and thanksgiving for all His kindness shown to them. Second, to lay before the Savior the distress and case of all who were known to them in or out of the Congregation.

Through the years, Moravian Churches everywhere kept prayer at the forefront of their actions. There was established the Monthly Concert for Prayer, on the first Monday of the month. This concert for prayer is held in all the provinces. In August, 1872, there was instituted a Moravian Prayer Union. As one looks at some of these meetings, some of these prayers, your eye scans across the pages and sees words like these, "Bless the congregations gathered from the heathen, in Labrador and Greenland, in South Africa and Australia, in North America and Central Asia, in Surinam and the Islands of the Western Sea. Own the labors and sustain the courage of our dear missionaries and their devoted wives, and enable them to commit their children to thy loving care for soul and body." (15)

The protection of the Moravian missionaries was counted to have been secured in the prayer closet. "When we consider the character of those tribes among whom labor has been carried on for a century and a half, it will seem surprising that no more Moravians have fallen by the hand of violence; and, when it is farther considered that the brethren and sisters who have been engaged in the foreign service number over two thousand, that most of them have crossed the ocean more than once, and that usually the voyages are attended by special perils, it must impress us that the sea holds no more of their dead to be given up on the resurrection morning. Only thirty are recorded as having suffered death by violence or accident." (16)

§

The Secret of Revival? Ultimately the answer to that lies in the mind and heart of Almighty God. However, as you trace revival across the centuries of church life, you begin to find certain items that head the list of things inherent in revival:

The Exaltation of Jesus Christ

The Centrality of the Cross of Christ

Love for the Brethren

Total Surrender

Prayer

May God grant that we survey these five items and be certain they are imbedded in our lives, so that we may experience true revival.

CHAPTER THIRTY-ONE

"MORAVIANS TODAY"

Moravians are still active in our world today. Their existence today can be traced to the motto of the Moravian Church down through the centuries. Their motto was instituted by Count Zinzendorf himself, "In essentials, unity; in nonessentials, liberty; in all things, love." (1) As the Moravians went out across the world in their missionary enterprises, it was never their goal to begin new churches, to establish a new denomination. Their primary goal was to win people to faith in Jesus Christ. There are many instances where the Moravians would win a number of people to Christ, then turn them over to an existing church to nurture them.

They were known by many names, the Hussites, beginning in the early 1400s, the Bohemian Brethren, the Unitas Fratrum, the Church of the Brethren, and the Moravians. By whatever name you call them, they were a group of people who were doing their best to believe the Bible as the Word of God, believe in Jesus Christ as Savior and Lord, and live according to the principles of Scripture.

This group marched on through the centuries, finally settling in Herrnhut, Germany in 1722. When the Holy Spirit came on their little church in 1727, they began to go out across the world with the message of Jesus Christ, crucified and risen from the dead.

The things Moravians believed had a deep impact on their ministry, their lives, and their future. The doctrinal beliefs of Moravians have stood firm across the years.

Salvation
God's will for salvation is revealed completely and clearly in the Bible, through the sacrifice of Jesus Christ on the cross.

Baptism
Infants, children, and adults are baptized. Through baptism the individual receives a pledge of the forgiveness of sin and admission into the covenant of God through the blood of Jesus Christ.

Jesus Christ
There is no salvation apart from Christ. He redeemed the whole of humanity by his death and resurrection and is present with us in the Word and the Sacrament.

Communion
The Moravian Church does not try to explain the mystery of this sacrament of Christ's presence in the bread and wine. Believers engage in an act of covenant with Christ as Savior and with other believers.

The Holy Spirit
The Holy Spirit is one of the three Persons of the Trinity, who directs and unites Christians and forms them into a church.

The Spirit calls each person individually to recognize his sin and accept redemption through Christ.

Priesthood of All Believers
The Moravian Church recognizes the priesthood of all believers, but does ordain ministers and deacons, as well as consecrates presbyters and bishops.

The Trinity
God is triune in nature: Father, Son, and Holy Spirit and is the only source of life and salvation.

Unity
The Moravian Church takes a firm stand for unity in the church, recognizing Christ as the sole head of the church, who is leading his scattered children toward unity. Moravians cooperate with other Christian denominations in worthwhile charitable ventures and respect the differences among Christian churches.

Sacraments
The Moravian Church recognizes two sacraments; baptism and communion. Baptism is done by sprinkling and, for infants, implies responsibility for the infant, parents and congregation. Youth and adults may be baptized at the time they make a profession of faith.

Communion
Communion is observed several times during the year, with

freedom given to individual churches as to how they present the elements of bread and wine. Praise and prayer are both done during the communion service, as well as the extending the right hand of fellowship at the beginning and the close of the service. All baptized adult Christians may take communion.

Worship Services

Music plays an important part in the Moravian services. The church has a tradition of brass and woodwind instruments, but piano, organ and guitars are all used. Most Moravian Churches has a "come as you are" dress code. (2)

§

One thing that has been passed down through the years in the Moravian Church is the "Moravian Daily Texts." This is a series of devotions, a Scripture passage that is to be read every day. The "Moravian Daily Texts" had its beginning with Count Zinzendorf in Herrnhut, Germany. Today, the "Moravian Daily Texts" are chosen in Herrnhut. For the United States, the "Daily Texts" are received in America, sent to a translator, printed and made available in every Moravian home. The important thing is that the texts are translated properly so that Moravians around the world are reading identical devotional material on any given day.

Today there are about one million members of the Moravian Church worldwide. The greatest number live in eastern Africa, especially in Tanzania. There are 80,000 Moravians in South Africa. Other major Moravian centers are in the U.S. Virgin Islands, Antigua, Jamaica, Tobago, Surinam, Guyana, St. Kitts, Honduras and Nicaragua. There is still a Moravian presence in London in Fetter Lane where John and Charles Wesley came to know Jesus Christ as Savior.

In North America, the Moravian Church is divided into four provinces: Northern (which includes five Canadian churches), Southern, Alaska, and Labrador.

The Northern Province has its headquarters in Bethlehem, Pennsylvania. In this province there are the following churches:

District of Columbia- 1 church
Maryland- 3 churches
New Jersey- 5 churches
New York- 11 churches
Ohio- 7 churches
Ontario- 1 church
Pennsylvania- 23 churches
California- 2 churches
Illinois- 1 church
Indiana- 1 church
Michigan- 3 churches
Minnesota- 7 churches
North Dakota- 4 churches
Wisconsin- 19 churches
Alberta, Canada- 8 churches

The headquarters of the Southern Province is located in Winston-Salem, North Carolina. In this province there are the following churches:

Florida- 9 churches

Georgia- 1 church

North Carolina- 48 churches

South Carolina- 1 church

Virginia- 2 churches (3)

The centuries have come and gone. We have looked at John Huss, Luke of Prague, Christian David, David Nitschmann, Count Ludwig von Zinzendorf, Peter Bohler and countless others who have shared the gospel of Jesus Christ in many parts of the world. When you really take a look at what the Moravians did, I, personally, come away with the distinct impression that I have had the opportunity to know Jesus Christ as my personal Savior because of the ministry of the Moravians. For, you see, if Peter Bohler had not shared Jesus Christ with John and Charles Wesley, then great revival may not have come to England, which would have meant that revival would not have spread to America, which would have left my country in the dark concerning the gospel of Jesus Christ. I give praise to the Lord for raising up the Moravians so that I could know Christ and Him crucified.

The secret of revival for the Moravians?

1. Prayer

2. Total Surrender to Jesus Christ

3. The Exaltation of Christ

4. The Centrality of the Cross of Christ

5. Love for the Brethren

—⁂—

May God grant that we may see great revival in our day. Please remember, "If My people, who are called by My name, shall humble themselves, and pray, and seek My face, and turn from their wicked ways, then I will hear from heaven, and will forgive their sin, and heal their land." (II Chronicles 7:14)

Following Pages:
End Notes and Bibliography

END NOTES

Chapter One:
"The Times of John Huss"

1   Hutton, J. E. "A History of the Moravian Church",
         BiblioBazaar, 2006
2   Ibid.
3   Ibid.
4   Ibid.
5   Ibid.
6   Moravian Archives
7   Hutton, J. E. "A History of the Moravian Church",
         BiblioBazaar, 2006

Chapter Two:
"After John Huss"

1   Hutton, J. E. "A History of the Moravian Church",
         BiblioBazaar, 2006

Chapter Three:
"The Apostle Peter of the 15th Century"

1   Hutton, J. E. "A History of the Moravian Church",
         BiblioBazaar, 2006

Chapter Four:
"The Beginning of the Church of the Brethren"

1   Hutton, J. E. "A History of the Moravian Church",
         BiblioBazaar, 2006
2   Ibid.

3   Ibid.
4   Ibid.

Chapter Five:
"Luke of Prague"
1   Hutton, J. E. "A History of the Moravian Church",
     BiblioBazaar, 2006
2   Ibid.

Chapter Six:
"A Bend in the Road"
1   Moravian Archives
2   Hutton, J. E. "A History of the Moravian Church",
     BiblioBazaar, 2006

Chapter Seven:
"The Bohemian Luther"
1   Hutton, J. E. "A History of the Moravian Church",
     BiblioBazaar, 2006
2   Ibid.
3   Ibid.
4   Ibid.

Chapter Eight:
"The Exodus to Poland"
1   Hutton, J. E. "A History of the Moravian Church",
     BiblioBazaar, 2006

Chapter Nine:
"Meanwhile, Back in Bohemia"
1　Hutton, J. E. "A History of the Moravian Church", BiblioBazaar, 2006
2　Ibid
3　Ibid.

Chapter Ten:
"The Brethren's Time of Peace"
1　Hutton, J. E. "A History of the Moravian Church", BiblioBazaar, 2006
2　Ibid.

Chapter Eleven:
"The Golden Age Turns to Nightmare"
1　Hutton, J. E. "A History of the Moravian Church", BiblioBazaar, 2006

Chapter Twelve:
"The Killing Begins"
1　Moravian Archives
2　Moravian Archives
3　Hutton, J. E. "A History of the Moravian Church", BiblioBazaar, 2006
4　Ibid.

Chapter Thirteen:
"The Church in Hiding"
1　Hutton, J. E. "A History of the Moravian Church",

BiblioBazaar, 2006
2   Ibid.

Chapter Fourteen:
"German Pietism"
1   Moravian Archives
2   Ibid.

Chapter Fifteen:
"Enter: Count Zinzendorf"
1   Hutton, J. E. "A History of the Moravian Church",
     BiblioBazaar, 2006, Page 166
2   Ibid. Page 170
3   Ibid. Page 172
4   Ibid. Page 175

Chapter Sixteen:
"From Servant Boy to Servant of the Lord"
1   Moravian Archives

Chapter Seventeen:
"Destination: Herrnhut"
1   Moravian Archives

Chapter Eighteen:
"Satan Arrives in Herrnhut"
1   Hutton, J. E. "A History of the Moravian Church",
     BiblioBazaar, 2006

Chapter Nineteen:
"Pentecost Comes to Herrnhut"

1   Moravian Archives: "The Brotherly Agreement
    of the Moravian Church"

2   Greenfield, John. "Power from on High",
    The World-Wide Revival Prayer Movement, Page 34

3   Ibid. Page 46

Chapter Twenty-Two:
"After the Moravian Pentecost"

1   Hutton, J. E. "A History of the Moravian Church",
    BiblioBazaar, 2006, Page 198

2   Ibid. Page 207

3   Ibid. Page 211

4   Ibid. Page 212

Chapter Twenty-Three:
"The Moravians and Missions"

1   Hutton, J. E. "A History of the Moravian Church",
    BiblioBazaar, 2006

2   Greenfield, John. "Power from on High", World-Wide
    Revival Prayer Movement, Page 70

Chapter Twenty-Four:
"The Gospel in the Caribbean Islands"

1   Hutton, J. E. "A History of the Moravian Church",
    BiblioBazaar, 2006, Page 216

2   Whately, Jane. "The Gospel in Bohemia"
    BiblioLife, Page 128

3   Thompson, Augustus. "Moravian Missions",
     Charles Scribner's Sons, New York, 1882, Page 81
4   Ibid. Page 84
5   Ibid. Page 85
6   Ibid. Page 92

Chapter Twenty-Five:
"The Gospel in South America"
1   Gorkie, A. C. "Christian Mission in Wrong Places,
     among Wrong Races, and in Wrong Hands", London,
     1871, Page 101
2   Thompson, Augustus. "Moravian Missions",
     Charles Scribner's Sons, New York, 1882, Page 134-35
3   Ibid. Page 141
4   Ibid. Page 149

Chapter Twenty-Six:
"The Gospel in Greenland"
1   Thompson, Augustus. "Moravian Missions",
     Charles Scribner's Sons, New York, 1882, Page 177
2   Ibid. Page 181
3   Hutton, J. E. "A History of the Moravian Church",
     BiblioBazaar, 2006, Page 220
4   Thompson, Augustus. "Moravian Missions",
     Charles Scribner's Sons, New York, 1882, Page 201

Chapter Twenty-Seven:
"The Gospel in America"
1   Hutton, J. E. "A History of the Moravian Church",

BiblioBazaar, 2006, Page 227

2   "The Journal of John Wesley"

3   Ibid.

4   Ibid.

5   Thompson, Augustus. "Moravian Missions, Charles Scribner's Sons, New York, 1882, Page 279

6   Loskiel's History, Part II, Page 14-15

7   Hutton, J. E. "A History of the Moravian Church", BiblioBazaar, 2006, Page 339

Chapter Twenty-Eight:
"The Gospel Everywhere"

1   Hoover, Peter. "Behold the Lamb", 2011, Page 174

Chapter Twenty-Nine:
"Soldiers in a Common Cause"

1   Thompson, Augustus. "Moravian Missions", Charles Scribner's Sons, New York, 1882, Page 177

2   Hutton, J. E. "A History of the Moravian Church", BiblioBazaar, 2006, Page 180

3   Thompson, Augustus. "Moravian Missions", Charles Scribner's Sons, New York, 1882, Page 34

4   Christian History, Issue 1

5   Spangenberg, August Gottlieb. "An Exposition of Christian Doctrine", London, Page 193-94

6   Hutton, J. E. "A History of the Moravian Church", BiblioBazaar, 2006, Page 383

7   Nitschmann, David. "Bethlehem Diary XVIII, Page 267-79

8   Hutton, J. E. "A History of the Moravian Church",
    BiblioBazaar, 2006, Page 288
9   Ibid.
10 Cennick, John. "An Account of a Late Riot At Exeter",
    London, J. Hart, 1745,   Page 3
11 Ibid. Page 4
12 Ibid. Page 6
13 The Journal of John Wesley, March 4, 1738
14 Hutton, J. E. "A History of the Moravian Church",
    BiblioBazaar, 2006, Page 295
15 Lockwood, John. "Memorials of the Life of
    Peter Bohler" Wesleyan Conference Office, London,
    1868. Page 47
16 Moravian Archives

Chapter Thirty:
"The Secret to Revival"

1   Allen, Brad. "Catch the Wind",
    Word Association Publishers, Tarentum,
    Pennsylvanian, 2002
2   Moravian Archives
3   Ibid.
4   Ibid.
5   Ibid.
6   Ibid.
7   Ibid.
8   Ibid.
9   Ibid.
10 Ibid.

11 Ibid.

12 Thompson, Augustus. "Moravian Missions",
    Charles Scribner's Sons, New York, 1882, Page 5

13 Ibid. Page 323

14 Christianity Today, "Zinzendorf and the Moravians",
    Issue 1, 1982

15 Thompson, Augustus, "Moravian Missions",
    Charles Scribner's Sons, New York, 1882, Page 480

16 Ibid. Page 481-82

Chapter Thirty-One:
"Moravians Today"

1   Moravian Archives

2   Moravian Church in North America Website

3   Ibid.

BIBLIOGRAPHY

Books:
Allen, Brad. "Catch the Wind".
Word Association Publishers,
Tarentum, Pennsylvania, 2002

Anonymous. "The Moravians in Labrador",
A public domain book

Atwood, Craig D. "Zinzendorf and the Holy Spirit."

Bethlehem Diary, Volume XVIII, 1758.
Moravian Archives

Berlin Discourse Number 16, April, 1738

Moravian Archives. "The Brotherly Agreement of the
Moravian Church."

Cennick, John. "An Account of a Late Riot at
Exeter", J. Hart, London, 1745

Curtis, A. K. "A Golden Summer"

Greenfield, John. "Power from on High", Hunt, Barnard
and Co, London, 1927

Friedberg Moravian Church, "The Ground of the Unity."

Huss, John. "Confession of Faith and Religion of the Barons and Nobles of the Kingdom of Bohemia presented to the most serene and invincible King of the Romans, Bohemia, etc. at Vienna, Austria in the year of our Lord, 1535

Hutton, J. E. "A History of the Moravian Church", BiblioBazaar, 2006

Kingsley, Charles. "At Last"

Lockwood, John. "Memorials of the Life of Peter Bohler", Wesleyan Conference Office, 1868

Loskie, George Henry. "History of the Mission of the Unity Brethren among the Indians in North America", Brethren's Society, London, 1794

"Luke of Prague", Moravian Archives in Bethlehem, Pennsylvania

"Moravian Church in America", Rolling Hills Moravian Church

"Moravian Church in North America", Moravian Archives

Taylor, Dean. ""The Moravian Mission Machine"

Thompson, Augustus. "Moravian Missions", Charles Scribner's Sons, London, 1882

Unknown. "The Moravians in Greenland" Leeaf Classics

Weber, Julie. "Zinzendorf's Pennsylvania Sermons"

Wesley, John. "The Journal of John Wesley"

Whately, Jane. "The Gospel in Bohemia", London, The Religious Tract Society, 1923

Video:
"Count Zinzendorf", Comenius Foundation

To order copies of book:
Brad Allen
3210 Timber Ridge Dr
Duncan, Oklahoma 73533
Phone: 580-467-0702
E-mail: bla20@cableone.net
Website: www.bradallen.faithweb.com

WA